Folk and Gypsy Magic

A Comprehensive Guide to Norse Paganism, Brujeria, Curanderismo, Jewish Magic, Kabbalah, Romani Witchcraft, and More

© **Copyright 2024 - All rights reserved.**

The content contained within this book may not be reproduced, duplicated, or transmitted without direct written permission from the author or the publisher.

Under no circumstances will any blame or legal responsibility be held against the publisher, or author, for any damages, reparation, or monetary loss due to the information contained within this book, either directly or indirectly.

Legal Notice:

This book is copyright protected. It is only for personal use. You cannot amend, distribute, sell, use, quote, or paraphrase any part, or the content within this book, without the consent of the author or publisher.

Disclaimer Notice:

Please note the information contained within this document is for educational and entertainment purposes only. All effort has been executed to present accurate, up-to-date, reliable, and complete information. No warranties of any kind are declared or implied. Readers acknowledge that the author is not engaging in the rendering of legal, financial, medical, or professional advice. The content within this book has been derived from various sources. Please consult a licensed professional before attempting any techniques outlined in this book.

By reading this document, the reader agrees that under no circumstances is the author responsible for any losses, direct or indirect, that are incurred as a result of the use of the information contained within this document, including, but not limited to, errors, omissions, or inaccuracies.

Your Free Gift
(only available for a limited time)

Thanks for getting this book! If you want to learn more about various spirituality topics, then join Mari Silva's community and get a free guided meditation MP3 for awakening your third eye. This guided meditation mp3 is designed to open and strengthen ones third eye so you can experience a higher state of consciousness. Simply visit the link below the image to get started.

https://spiritualityspot.com/meditation

Or, Scan the QR code!

Table of Contents

PART 1: FOLK MAGIC...1
   INTRODUCTION 2
   CHAPTER 1: FOLK MAGIC BASICS 4
   CHAPTER 2: AFRICAN SPIRITUALITY 12
   CHAPTER 3: BRUJERIA AND CURANDERISMO 24
   CHAPTER 4: SCOTTISH WITCHCRAFT 34
   CHAPTER 5: DRUIDRY AND CELTIC MAGIC 42
   CHAPTER 6: NORSE PAGANISM 51
   CHAPTER 7: JEWISH MAGIC AND THE KABBALAH 60
   CHAPTER 8: SACRED PLANTS AND HERBS 70
   CHAPTER 9: SIGNS, SYMBOLS, AND CHARMS 80
   CHAPTER 10: YOUR FOLK MAGIC SPELLBOOK 100
   CONCLUSION 109
PART 2: GYPSY MAGIC..111
   INTRODUCTION 112
   CHAPTER 1: GYPSY WITCHCRAFT BASICS 114
   CHAPTER 2: LORE, CODES, AND BELIEFS 124
   CHAPTER 3: GYPSY OMENS AND CUSTOMS............................131
   CHAPTER 4: SIGNS AND SYMBOLS 139
   CHAPTER 5: HOW TO MAKE AMULETS AND TALISMANS 148
   CHAPTER 6: MAGICAL HERBS AND PLANTS - A LITTLE HERBAL GRIMOIRE 156
   CHAPTER 7: GYPSY TAROT I. THE CARDS 166

CHAPTER 8: GYPSY TAROT II - READING THE CARDS 175
CHAPTER 9: OTHER TYPES OF GYPSY DIVINATION 187
CHAPTER 10: GYPSY SPELLS AND CHARMS 197
CONCLUSION 204
HERE'S ANOTHER BOOK BY MARI SILVA THAT YOU MIGHT LIKE 205
YOUR FREE GIFT (ONLY AVAILABLE FOR A LIMITED TIME) 206
REFERENCES 207

Part 1: Folk Magic

The Ultimate Guide to Norse Paganism, Brujeria, Curanderismo, Scottish Witchcraft, Jewish Magic, Kabbalah, Druidry, and African American Spirituality

Introduction

When you think of magical practices, European and Middle Eastern traditions often come to mind. These usually encompass Wiccan magic practices, Paganism, Druidism, and other neopagan systems. However, throughout history, magical practices have been a part of numerous other cultures. So, to imagine that all magic practices boil down to pagan concepts is a tempting yet misdirected notion. For that reason, it's critical to include vibrant folk magic traditions such as Voodoo, Hoodoo, Curanderismo, Brujeria, and Kabbalah magic, alongside Celtic and Norse magic. Most folk magic books out there only focus on well-known cultures that practice magic, omitting the less common ones. By contrast, this book will highlight each culture and the associated magical practices in extensive detail.

Paganism, witchcraft, and other magical practices have been around for much longer than one might think. Surprisingly, these practices are now more popular than ever before. False notions of witchcraft and magical practices have been common throughout history. In the past, those suspected of engaging in it faced dangerous consequences, excommunication, and even death. Today, fortunately, many magical practices are carried out openly without fear. Whether it's Jewish mystic and occult teachings or Celtic practices, many people are eagerly learning the practices and teachings of these ancient belief systems.

Whether you want to learn about the magic practices of Celtic culture or wish to familiarize yourself with Scottish witchcraft, this book will be the perfect guide for you. For someone interested in magic practices but unsure where to start this journey, reading this book will provide you with just enough knowledge about the various folk magic traditions to make an informed decision. Even if you're interested in a single culture, a lot of information is provided for each one, along with its fundamental concepts and traditions.

The opening chapter will guide you in choosing which folk magic culture you identify with most, while the following chapters will cover each specific folk magic culture. Every chapter details the history and development of that culture and the belief system they follow. The traditions and holidays observed by these cultures will also be discussed in detail to give you a complete idea of what it's like in practice. While you might feel that a single chapter cannot cover a particular culture comprehensively, it provides all the necessary fundamentals to discover and connect with it.

This book does not claim to make you a master of folk magic within a few weeks. Instead, it promises that once you've read it, you'll have enough knowledge about each kind of folk magic to decide based on your preference. The best part? We've included a section dedicated at the end of each chapter with self-reflective questions to help you decide which culture you feel attracted to intuitively. Without further ado, if you're ready to delve into the world of folk magic and uncover its deepest secrets, let's get started!

Chapter 1: Folk Magic Basics

As you study magic and navigate through this fascinating topic, the term "folk magic" will surely come up. As it happens, there's always a great deal of curiosity around folk magic and its practitioners. People often confuse it with witchcraft, and some even believe practitioners are necessarily religious and worship a specific lord. Others believe that people who practice this magic are polytheistic or nature worshippers.

Some believe that people who practice this magic are polytheistic or nature worshippers.
https://www.pexels.com/photo/woman-in-traditional-wear-11960754/

There's a reason why folk magic is often associated with religion and gods. Modern practitioners working with magico-religion have adopted folk magic in their practices, resulting in many misconceptions about this practice. However, folk magic is different from magical practices associated with religion, such as Druidry, Wicca, and Shamanism. In this first chapter, we will clear any misconceptions you may have about folk magic and explain what makes it different from other types of magic.

Folk Magic Explained

Despite being one of the oldest magical practices in the world, folk magic has managed to adapt to modern practices and other cultures. Essentially, folk magic is an umbrella term that encompasses various magical practices. What distinguishes these practices from other types of magic is that they're all practiced by the common folk. In other words, it isn't a type of ceremonial magic that requires specific skills or a professional practitioner.

Folk magic differs from other types of magic mainly due to its practicability. It focuses on practical issues and helping people and the community. For example, it can help women struggling with fertility, bring good luck, help people find love, drive evil spirits away, cure diseases, and help retrieve lost objects. Since this type of magic was practiced by common folks who were often illiterate back then, it relied on oral traditions, and the spells were simple enough for them to memorize. Working with folk magic isn't complicated since most of the materials needed are common and include wood, nails, plants, eggshells, stones, coins, and twine.

The History of Folk Magic

By definition, folk practices are old, maybe even ancient. For instance, Scottish folk magic can be traced back to the old way of life. Different cultures influenced this particular tradition, including the Saxons, Angles, Gaelic, Pictish, Norman, and Norse. It borrowed from ancient mythologies and traditions until it formed its own combination of folklore and myth. Although folk magic has developed, become independent, and created its own folklore and mythology, it still holds on to its original system of culture and politics.

Luckily, folk magic hasn't disappeared in the confines of history, as many literal folks were able to preserve it by writing it down. Today, we know about their rituals, prayers, practices, beliefs, festivals, celebrations, and songs. For example, one of the more interesting practices passed down to us is "Ranns." The folks sang these special songs before bedtime, when waking up, when sowing seeds, and before picking plants.

The Main Characteristics of Folk Magic

Folk magic has many distinguishable traits. For starters, it's a simple practice available to the greatest number, it's often practiced orally, and it helps with issues that people deal with in their daily lives. Practitioners also customize the rituals and items they use based on the target of their spell. This is meant to link the target and symbols together.

Generally speaking, spells in folk magic use various elements from nature, like water, stones, and plants. For instance, practitioners use stones to help the ill, tie pieces of cloth onto sacred wells for faster healing, and use Holy stones as tools to see into the world of the spirits. Another trait that distinguishes folk magic is that it can be practiced with any type of readily available tool. Unlike many other practices, rituals also don't play a great role in folk magic.

That is the beauty of folk magic – it's straightforward, and since it's the magic of the common folk, it doesn't require anything special or over the top. Every practitioner can choose the methods they see fit. This type of practical magic is ideal for normal daily needs and can be practiced with minimal effort.

Folk Magic vs. Witchcraft and Ceremonial Magic

As established, folk magic differs from Druidry, Wicca, and Witchcraft. Each of these types of magic has its own beliefs and traditions. However, all were heavily influenced by folk magic. More often than not, people treat witchcraft as an umbrella term that comprises all types of magic. However, witchcraft is its own type and differs from other types of magic, especially folk magic.

It's hard to compare folk magic with witchcraft since folk practitioners are not interested in witches. In fact, they consider them evil. This is something significant in folk magic beliefs that's useful to remember if you ever encounter folk practitioners. Some practitioners, especially Scottish ones, consider it offensive to compare or affiliate them with witches. Unlike witchcraft, folk magic isn't associated with or influenced by religion. They don't worship a specific deity and don't have to follow a specific set of beliefs to practice this type of magic. Since folk magic is ancient, its approaches and ideas haven't borrowed anything from modern religions. However, several folk magic practices preserved in literary works were later Christianized.

It's common knowledge how magic and those who practiced it or were suspected of practicing it were treated in Europe back in the day. Some even claimed that Christians believed folk magic was the same as witchcraft and prosecuted its practitioners. However, there's no factual truth to these claims. Witchcraft and folk magic are often opposites. Folk practitioners were respected in their communities, as the main purpose of their magic was to help and heal people. On the other hand, Witchcraft didn't serve the community and was often regarded as evil or harmful.

Witchcraft, Wicca, and other types of magic have borrowed various techniques from ceremonial magic, such as invoking gods and goddesses or forming circles to practice magic. By contrast, folk magic doesn't use any of these techniques or borrow from ceremonial magic. Ceremonial magic is also known for its use of rituals, another aspect that distinguishes it from folk magic. Unlike folk magic, practitioners of ceremonial magic need certain tools and accessories for practice, referred to as ceremonial weapons.

Cunning Folk

If you type "folk magic" on any search engine, you'll find the words "cunning folk" frequently coming up. Who were the cunning folk, and how were they associated with folk magic? The term cunning folk describes diviners, folk magic practitioners, and healers who lived in Europe during the Middle Ages, all through the 20th century. For centuries, the cunning folk worked to help their communities by providing various services that often involved magic. These folks were hard workers who did everything they could to help their communities and even neighboring ones. They would travel for miles to help the sick, provide a sympathetic ear and a shoulder to cry on to those in need, and use their magic to help the afflicted. Any modern-day magic practitioner is influenced by cunning folk. These wise men and women were highly respected and known for their immense knowledge.

As it happens, cunning folks didn't name themselves as such. It was historians who referred to them by that unflattering denomination. Cunning folks played a significant role in the magic world, and everyone knew at least one cunning folk. They were treated differently from others who practiced magic, as they weren't witches or associated with witchcraft. People saw their magic as helpful rather than evil.

Practicing folk magic allowed these gifted individuals to help others and find solutions to the problems common people encountered. This is why the term is often associated with folk magic because many of its practitioners were cunning folks and used their magic benevolently. However, unlike other folk magic practitioners, the cunning folk were literate. The folk magic practiced by this group traveled beyond Europe and became popular in other parts of the world, notably North America.

Folk Magic Cultural Path

Now that you're familiar with the concept of folk magic, you probably wonder how you can start practicing. Although folk magic doesn't seem complicated, since it's the magic of the people, it does have one major challenge beginners often encounter. Folk magic practitioners struggle to find the right cultural path for them. In this dedicated section, we will focus on folk magic cultural paths so you can choose the one that suits you best.

Hoodoo

Hoodoo is one of the traditional folk magic and rootwork practices. The word "Hoodoo" doesn't mean the same thing to everyone but depends on the type of practice and practitioners. It's often referred to as rootwork or conjures. Hoodoo originated in various African practices during the 19th century. It found its way to the United States, merging with popular magical practices, including European folklore and Native American. While this syncretism of practices may seem rather uncommon, it was the foundation from which contemporary Hoodoo evolved.

Since Hoodoo's birthplace in Africa, many of its practitioners are African-Americans. However, people from different cultures and backgrounds follow this practice as well. Some Hoodoo practitioners have learned this practice from their relatives, as it's often passed down from one generation to the next. The practice of traditional Hoodoo has remained the same ever since it originated.

Since Hoodoo is a branch of folk magic, most of its spells are practical ones that involve lust, love, and money. Although Hoodoo isn't a pagan practice and its followers don't worship any deities, some highly revere their ancestors. That said, a large number of its practitioners are devout Christians. In some regions in the United States, people practice mountain magic, which they usually refer to as Hoodoo. Practitioners of this type of Hoodoo incorporate various tools into their practice, like charms, amulets, and omens.

It's essential to note that Hoodoo and Voodoo are two distinct practices. They're easy to confuse due to similar spellings, but the two couldn't be more different. Voodoo revolves around religious practices and worshiping various deities that aren't associated with folk magic. However, they share the same background, as both originated in Africa.

If you plan on practicing Hoodoo magic, you should begin by reading about the history of Africans and the struggles and trauma they faced due to their enslavement.

Pow-wow

Often referred to as "braucherei," Pow-wow is another type of folk magic. This practice focuses on healing the sick and making remedies. Americans of German descent who lived in Pennsylvania were the first to practice this type of magic. The charms, remedies, and rituals found in Pow-wow originated in Europe and later found their way to the United States, specifically Pennsylvania. This interesting name comes from the Algonquian language and refers to a healing ritual.

Incidentally, a popular practice among Native Americans goes by the same name, which often causes confusion among magical practitioners. However, Pow-wow folk magic is different from its namesake. The European settlers who mingled with Native Americans adopted the term Pow-wow, which described a healing ritual. The Native American Pow-wow involves a gathering of people from various cultures where they dance, sing, celebrate, and practice rituals. However, both practices share their etymology. Nowadays, practitioners prefer the term braucherei to differentiate between folk magic Pow-wow and the Native American version.

Back in the 17th century, many Native Americans lived in Pennsylvania. Various tribes resided on-site, while other tribes visited the region occasionally. In the late 17th century and throughout the 18th century, European settlers made their way to Pennsylvania. Some of these settlers were German, and these newcomers had their own religion, beliefs, and traditions. As a result, their magical practices were mainly religious. Religion played a significant role in their practices as they highly revered the Catholic Saints, and prayers and blessings were a great part of their lives. Healing practices often involved herbal remedies, invoking a god, and Holy objects. They used and continue to use sacred symbols to protect themselves, their families, and their homes. Farmers still decorate their barns using various hex signs to invoke protection.

The religious influence over Pow-wow didn't die down over the years. In fact, practitioners have relied on the Bible and incorporated various verses in their practices. Magic and religion were very much integrated, as practitioners believed that only God could provide healing. According to their beliefs, there was no better or more effective way to practice healing folk magic than scripture. Pow-wow practitioners often used charms and spells that belonged to the Catholics who lived in medieval Europe. Back then, these Catholics used these spells and charms as protection against evil magic and witchcraft. For example, they used them to protect their cattle, stop bleeding, treat burns, protect against thefts, cure fevers, and as a good luck charm before a court.

Pow-wow is still a common practice favored by many practitioners to this day. Male practitioners are called Braucher, while female practitioners are called Braucherin. In other communities around Pennsylvania, they're referred to as Pow-wowers or Pow-wow doctors, owing to their status as healers. Pow-wow, like folk magic, relied mainly on oral tradition. Spells, rituals, charms, and prayers were never written down but passed down orally from one generation to the next. Male practitioners taught female practitioners, and vice-versa. Practitioners of this type of magic believed that only students who wanted to help others and make a difference in the world should learn Pow-wow. They memorize their prayers and rituals and vow to share them with those they believe were chosen by God to provide healing to the sick.

There are certain rules every Pow-wow practitioner should abide by:
- Under no circumstances should practitioners get paid for their services
- You should never reveal the name of the person who introduced you to Pow-wow
- To practice Pow-wow, you should be a Christian who worships the Christian God and follow the teachings of the Bible

Now that you're familiar with folk magic's main types and cultural paths, you can choose the one you feel most connected to. If you can't decide, you can apply eclectic magic and mix both traditions. That said, before deciding on a cultural path, it's wise to investigate your family tree to learn more about your cultural heritage. This step is necessary to help you choose the appropriate culture and put you on the right path. Belief is another strong tool that can guide you toward the right choice. In fact, belief and intention are essential elements in all types of magic, including folk magic. Intention, belief, and exploring your family tree are the main factors that can help anyone decide which culture to follow.

Choosing a cultural path is only the beginning of your journey. The next step is learning as much as possible about that culture. So, conduct further research by reading about your chosen culture's history, beliefs, customs, and traditions. While you can find many helpful resources online, it's best to enlist the help of practitioners in your community. You can talk to them, seek their advice, ask them questions, and give yourself a chance to learn firsthand from experienced practitioners. If any relatives are practitioners, they can also provide useful information about your family tree and various cultural paths.

This chapter is only the beginning of a personal, fascinating journey. The upcoming chapters will each cover the most widespread folk practices. The beneficial knowledge you'll come across will come in handy as you embark on your journey as a magic folk practitioner.

Magic can be a force for good or evil, depending on your chosen practice and how you plan on using it. Folk magic has proven to be a force for good over the centuries. People eager to help others and serve their community practice this magic and try to set themselves apart from witchcraft or any type of magic that doesn't benefit humanity or the greater good. Folk magic is the magic of the common folk, where healers devote their lives to easing people's pain, providing comfort, and ensuring their safety.

Chapter 2: African Spirituality

African spirituality is a broad umbrella that includes numerous traditions with several customs and spiritual beliefs. This chapter will delve into the basics of African spirituality. In this chapter, you'll learn about the origins of African spirituality and how various external forces influenced our modern perception of this system. You'll come across a few of Africa's most popular principal traditions and belief systems and understand their characteristics and main beliefs. Finally, you'll learn about the African pantheon, its most popular deities, and the most common methods of worship.

African spirituality is a broad umbrella that includes numerous traditions with several customs and spiritual beliefs.

https://www.pexels.com/photo/person-holding-lighted-candle-in-dark-room-6144036/

The Origins of African Spirituality

African spirituality is the melting pot of numerous cultures, nations, and traditions. It combines all that is natural and supernatural. Even as Islam and Christianity arrived on the continent, practitioners of African spirituality managed to get around these doctrines by incorporating them into their spiritual system with their deities and beliefs. Despite the continent's exceptional diversity, it still maintains some intrinsic similarities.

Since Africa was subject to colonialism throughout the centuries, African deities, folklore, legends, traditions, and beliefs were sullied, often forcefully, by outsiders. However, in most cases, natives were able to keep some parts of their practices intact. Many of the ancient core African beliefs are still prominent to this day.

Most African spiritual systems believe in the existence of one supreme god. For them, this divine force reigns over all living beings and non-living objects in all of the universe and the heavens. This god is also thought to be the ruler of the deities and spirits in the spiritual realm. They also believe in ancestor veneration, which is why the elderly are treated with the utmost respect. African spirituality suggests that there's an afterlife, which explains why practitioners conduct animal sacrifice after someone passes. They believe it allows the deceased to easily journey into the ancestral realm.

Many African cultures also conduct rites of passage and celebratory rituals for birth, entering adulthood, and death. When individuals enter puberty, they are celebrated with an initiation phase that includes rituals, passing tribal secrets and knowledge on to them, and male circumcision. Folklore typically approaches witchcraft with amazement, regarding it with a level of caution and fear as well. Non-practitioners usually use the term "witch doctor" to refer to spiritual practitioners, prophets, shamans, and traditional healers. However, in African culture, there is a great distinction between these entities and practices like black magic, sorcery, and witchcraft.

Several African spiritual systems are influenced and even based on Africanized versions of foreign world religions. African religious origins majorly rely on oral transmissions. It would be challenging to successfully portray oral-literary traditions in written form because they are not novel-like but rather take after animated plays. The messages would be grasped more effectively via performances instead of written stories. These pieces would lose their meaning, overtones, subtleties, vividness, and clarity if not accompanied by traditional dances, sound, voice, facial expressions, and body language.

There aren't any written ancient texts to guide modern practitioners through spiritual practices. They only conducted rituals and practiced oral transmissions, often done secretly after Christianity and Islam swept across the continent. Unfortunately, many foreign historical writers aimed to glorify their achievements and display their self-proclaimed moral superiority by depicting ancient African spirituality practices as savage, barbarian, sinful, and uncivilized.

For years, this was the world's perception of African spirituality, as there were no countering opinions from the practitioners themselves. Ancient African nations were subject to genocides and cruelty from outsiders who went on religious and colonial conquests.

Ancient African spiritualists didn't have to record their beliefs in writing because each group had its own expert storytellers who passed the practice down through generations. Trained storytellers acted as the scribes and priests of the time. They educated people about the heritage and history of their belief system to perpetuate it.

Although this system worked for centuries, it became a problem when the tribes started breaking away from each other. Only a few old traces of history remained with them. For instance, the ancient South African Nguni peoples only know that their ancestors were from the "north" and resided near the great lakes. The more they split up and traveled further away, the shorter and vaguer their stories became. Their history was starting to be replaced by newer events.

It's believed that the myths, tales, and deities of Africans spiritually arose during that time. During this period, people were forced to think more pragmatically and reflect on their experiences. They began using animal metaphors and symbols to teach moral lessons, myths, origin stories, deities, and belief systems. They also used storytelling to explain the origins of the world and creation and why everything is exactly the way it is.

The elderly instructed their extended family all about etiquette and moral lessons. Another reason the elderly were esteemed members of society is that they took up the role of community and family philosophers, advisors, and mentors. Even kings and tribe chiefs created councils that comprised elderly members for personal guidance and advice.

According to African culture, spirituality relates to every aspect of life. It can't be set apart from the mundane. Some researchers today reject this idea and suggest that diaspora Africans influenced ancient traditions with modern religious perceptions. However, in reality, we don't know how accurate our knowledge of ancient African myths and deities is. Storytellers perform generational stories the way they were taught. No one can guarantee that intentional changes were made and details were lost over the years. Besides, the evolution of dialects makes it difficult to trace the exact origins of these tales, along with African deities.

Main Traditions in African Spirituality

The following are some of the main traditions in African spirituality:

Kemetism

Kemetism is the revived form of the ancient Egyptian belief system known as Egyptian Neopaganism or Neterism. There are numerous groups of practitioners of Kemetic spirituality, each of which takes on a different spiritual approach.

The term "Kemetism" is derived from the word Kemet, the ancient Egyptian name for Egypt. Practitioners of this religion aim to practice ancient Egyptian spiritual rituals and beliefs. Ancient Egyptian spirituality is an extremely complex topic that many historians still haven't gotten to grips with. That said, the practitioners of Kemetism completely trust what they understand.

The core belief of Kemetism is the concept of Ma'at, which is the idea of divine balance. It's believed to be the guiding and driving force of the universe. Ma'at, the goddess, provides 42 laws that touch upon ethical and moral guidelines that a person should follow to be rebirthed in the afterlife. They also believe in Netjer, who is considered the only supreme being. According to ancient Egyptian mythology, all deities in the pantheon are manifestations of this supreme god.

Some Kemetic beliefs are highly controversial. For instance, while some practitioners believe that it's a polytheistic religion, which allows them to worship several gods, others suggest that it's a monotheistic belief system. This debate is the result of Netjer's nature. While he is a single supreme god, he still has several manifestations. Many Kemetic individuals also believe in ancestral veneration and often pray to their ancestors for guidance. Anyone can become Kemetic, as it doesn't require a specific initiation procedure.

Vodou

Also known as Voodoo or Vodoun, Vodou is a religion that combines native African spiritual beliefs and Roman Catholicism. The native African portion of the belief system comes from the religion of the West African Dahomey people. This belief system is currently practiced in New Orleans, Haiti, and other regions in the Caribbean.

Vodou started when African slaves brought their traditional beliefs with them to the "New World." However, since their owners prohibited them from maintaining their spiritual practices, they resorted to finding their gods in Catholic saints. They also used the imagery found in the Catholic Church to practice their native rituals. Vodou practitioners can choose to be Christians but generally adhere to the Catholic denomination; in that case, they may consider spirits and saints to be the same thing.

Vodou practitioners are monotheistic and believe in a single supreme god, known as Bondye. They also believe in the existence of lesser prominence beings, known as the Iwa. These are divided into the families of Ghede, Rada, and Petro, who are more involved in daily life. The Iwa and humans have a reciprocal connection, where the Iwa offer practitioners their assistance in exchange for food and offerings. They also believe in the existence of the afterlife. They think that a person's souls linger around until they experience rebirth after their death. If you wish to practice Voodoo, you need to engage in an extensive initiation period.

Santeria

Like Vodou, Santeria is a syncretic religion. It blends Yoruban spirituality, which comes from West Africa, traditional Caribbean influences, and aspects of Catholicism. It was also created when enslaved Africans were sent to work in the Caribbean.

Enslaved people also deemed it safer to worship saints as symbols of their ancestral Yoruban orishas or divine entities. According to Yoruban traditions, the orishas are messengers between the divine realm and the world of humans. This belief system relies on magical practices to invoke the orishas via divination methods, ritualistic practices, sacrifices, possession, and trances.

Many Americans practice Santeria today with the guidance of a high priest, especially when ceremonies or rituals are conducted. Before they are initiated, a Santero or high priest must undergo a testing period and meet certain requirements, including counseling and practicing divination and herbalism. The orishas are the ones who determine whether the candidate is a good fit for the priesthood.

The Orishas include Elegua (a messenger between humans and the divine), Yemaya (the essence of motherhood), Babalu Aye (the "Father of the World"), Chango (the embodiment of sexuality and masculine energy), and Oya, the guardian of those who have passed on. Each of these Orishas is the Santerian equivalent of a prominent Catholic figure or saint.

Santeria doesn't concern itself much with the afterlife. Rather, it focuses on the present moment and natural forces. Each of the Santerian deities represents a certain aspect or element of nature, like air, or a human trait, like power. To practice Santeria, you must complete a series of initiation rites.

The African Pantheon

The term "African Pantheon" comprises numerous tribes, belief systems, and deities. Most African spiritual belief systems have their own pantheons. For instance, the Vodou pantheon consists of 8 deities - Legba, Ayizan, Damballah, Egwe, Zaka, Egou, Guede, and Rzulie (Freda) Dahomey. Some religions believe in one supreme deity, like Juok, Roog, Olodumare, Nyame, and Chukwu, and they all generally possess similar traits. Since we cannot include all African gods in this chapter, we've gathered ten of the most powerful African deities. This section is a good starting point for the African pantheons and can give insight into the characteristics of significant African deities.

Sango

Sango is the Orisha of thunder. He is known for his ability to strike anyone who commits a crime with thunder and lightning. If the criminal is a thief, then the item they stole would be placed down on their chest, then they are struck down. Besides being considered the most powerful African god, he is among the most popular across the globe. Sango is the deity of numerous affairs, including maintaining social order, vengeance, and protection. He is believed to announce his presence by instigating a thunderstorm.

Nana Buluku

Nana Buluku is an African goddess and the Fon's people supreme Goddess. Although the Fon comes from the Ewes of Togo and Benin, Nana Buluku's prominence extends far beyond the border of these regions. While the Yorubas call her by that name, the Igbos refer to her as Olisabuluwa. She is believed to be the mother of the twin god of the Sun and the Moon, Mawu-Lisa.

Mawu-Lisa

Mawu-Lisa is a twin deity believed to be both female and male. Their Mawu aspect is the deity of the Moon, and Lisa is the deity of the Sun. They are responsible for maintaining order in the world.

Alekwu

Alekwu is one of the gods the Northern Nigerian Idoma peoples worship. He is a powerful deity known for settling disputes, protecting, and keeping social order. It's believed that this deity can hunt down and murder his enemy in one to three weeks. He is a feared punisher to those who commit or serve as accomplices to any crime. His followers believe that he is omnipresent, meaning that distance won't stop him from protecting or punishing people.

Inkosazana

Also known as Nomkhubuluwana, Inkosazana is the Zulu deity of agriculture and fertility. Her followers refer to her as the "Mermaid," as they believe she resides in water and manifests herself in that form and in the form of other animals. She is the protector of all and makes her presence known only to those who are pure at heart. She appears in dreams, misty clouds, and foggy waters and heals those who are ill.

Sho'risdal

This Berber goddess is a very compassionate being. She is believed to be the mother of abundance and life. The change of seasons is said to be instigated by her mood swings. Ironically, this deity of life and bounty is the wife of Vyinsul, the deity of death.

Ngai

The Kikuyus consider Ngai to be the god of all creation. He lives on African mountains and manifests himself through natural and celestial entities like the stars, moon, wind, rain, and sun. The Kikuyus also believe he lives in fig trees, which is why they make sacrifices for him there. Ngai is also believed to be responsible for human deaths.

Heka

Heka is among the earliest ancient Egyptian gods. He performed magic and healed people. He also pioneered the caduceus symbol, the popular image of two snakes swirling around a pole, which portrayed his power.

This symbol is now associated with the Greek god Hermes.

Mamlambo

Mamlambo is the South African and Zulu goddess of the rivers. She is thought to manifest as a giant snake that lives in the water. She has the power to grant wealth but is also able to cast horrid misfortunes. It's believed that Mamlambo feeds on the brains and faces of her victims.

Achamán

The Guanches people of Tenerife Island followed Achamán, the supreme god. He is considered the creator of air, land, and fire. He is responsible for breathing life into all creatures. Although he lives somewhere way above, he often descends to Earth to get in touch with his creations.

Eshu

Eshu is the African god of trickery and mischief, similar to the popular Norse god Loki. Unlike other trickster gods in various mythologies worldwide, Eshu is neither evil nor malicious. He doesn't spend his days playing tricks, nor does he enjoy mankind's suffering. Eshu acts as a messenger traveling between the physical and other worlds. This divine trickster has a devilish side, though. If a person or another deity doesn't acknowledge his presence, he is known to react unkindly toward them. He prefers offerings like tobacco.

Ogun

Ogun is the African god of war and iron. He is known as a warrior and always carries some of the finest weapons in heaven and earth. He exercises his role as the god of war and iron by blessing the weapons. According to African mythology, Ogun was the one who taught mankind how to make weapons using iron. He doesn't have a say in what a person chooses to do with these weapons. Ogun is a deity who doesn't interfere in the affairs of mankind. Many people pray to him and celebrate him in a festival every year.

Oshun

Oshun is the African goddess of the river. She is one of Shango's wives and the one closest to his heart. This river goddess is highly revered among the African people as they believe she has bestowed them with the Niger River, one of their most significant rivers. She blesses her people by keeping the rivers clean and ensuring they never run out of fish. This shows how much she cares about mankind. Oshun is also associated with childbirth and fertility. She is always depicted, showing her motherly and caring side.

Oya

Oya is the goddess of the weather and also one of Shango's wives. She is associated with the wind and has power over the clouds as well. She is one of the most powerful deities, as she can create cyclones and hurricanes. The African people believe that she causes destruction with Shango during thunderstorms. Oya also plays a role in the spirit realm as she provides help to the spirits of the dead as they begin their journey into the otherworld.

Yemaya

Yemaya is the African goddess of the ocean and the mother of all living things. Similar to Oshun, Yemayais is a caring mother, and she is fiercely protective of her children. In fact, she is the mother of all living beings. When someone is sad, she is always there for them, providing comfort and taking away their pain. Women who suffer from fertility issues often pray to her. She is a patient and loving goddess who rarely gets angry. However, when she does, she becomes a force for destruction. Thanks to her immense power and status, Yemaya is highly revered.

Modjaji

Modjaji is the goddess of rain, meaning she has the power to make the skies rain or prevent it and cause drought. She is one of the oldest goddesses, but the African people believe that her spirit lives in a young woman, and she now walks among them.

Oba

Another of Shango's wives, Oba, is the orisha of manifestation and water. Although she is a goddess, she still experiences human emotions. She was jealous of how much Shango loved Oshun. She went to her and asked why Shango loved her more than his other wives. Oshun was cunning and told Oba that she cut her ear and then made it into a powder-like substance to add to Shango's food. Oba believed Oshun's false story and did the same thing. However, when Shango found out, he sent her to earth. She turned into a river that was named after her.

Obaluaye

Obaluaye is the orisha of miracles and healing in African mythology. He is highly revered among his people, yet they are also terrified of him. Obaluaye can heal any ailments, but he can just as easily curse those who anger him. He can cure any disease, but he usually focuses on dying patients.

Obatala

Obatala is the father of the sky, the creator of mankind, and Yemaya's husband. He is a merciful god who represents purity and peace. Obatala is fair, which is why the orishas often seek his help and wisdom during conflicts. In African mythology, the people believed that all mankind's heads belonged to him since he was the creator.

Traditional Methods of Worship

Each belief system comes with a unique set of rites, rituals, practices, and methods of worship. However, most share the following characteristics:

Sacrifices

African spiritual systems often include the practice of sacrifices, which requires slaughtering an animal, bird, and sometimes even a human to honor a deity. Practitioners mindfully select their sacrifice to offer their bloodshed to appease a deity. The animals sacrificed must be of one solid color and are given back to a deity as a sign of appreciation for everything that they have done for them.

Sacrifices are considered an act of thankfulness or gratefulness. People also conduct sacrifices to earn god's forgiveness after committing wrongdoing. Sacrifices are thought to make a deity help their followers during challenging periods in life and serve as an invitation for the deity to partake in family and social gatherings. They can help practitioners maintain a good relationship with their deities and ask them to prevent perils such as floods, droughts, and epidemics.

Sacrifices are also conducted during rites of passage like birth, initiation, adulthood, marriage, and death. It was also believed that sacrifices could help alleviate the intensity of disasters and were commonly made after abundant harvests and before wars. Sacrifices weren't uncommon in the selection process of leaders, as well as cleansing and reconciliation ceremonies.

Heads of families, practitioners of medicines, and priests were the only elected members of society to conduct sacrifices. They have to accompany the process with prayers.

Offerings

Offerings are another means of worship. These require practitioners to provide their deity with milk, honey, or other food and beverage items. Offerings should be mindfully selected to suit the liking and preferences of the deity being worshiped.

Singing and Dancing

Practitioners frequently perform native songs and dances during communal worship. This practice serves to honor and thank a deity and strengthen the performer's emotional connection with them. Practitioners supplement their performances with drums, musical instruments, and hand clapping. Singing and dancing help instill a sense of community and solidarity among practitioners.

Prayers

Prayers are verbal interactions with a deity and are often short and straightforward. Most religious groups pray during significant occasions. One can pray while standing, prostrating, raising a hand, kneeling, bowing, or facing a specifically identified direction.

Invocations

Invocations are brief, formal, and concise forms of prayers. One may use this act of worship to address god, ask them for guidance, request their help, and more.

Blessings

Blessings are often conducted by elders and incorporate aspects of prayer. According to some belief systems, a person doing the blessing is doing so on behalf of a deity.

Salutations

As the name suggests, this method of worship involves addressing and saluting a god. For instance, a salutation would be "Dear God," etc.

Questions for Self-Reflection

- Do I have any African ancestors?
- Which African deities resonate with me the most?
- How do I feel about the mixing of different religious and cultural traditions?

Now that you've read this chapter, you have enough knowledge about African spirituality to determine whether this is the right belief system for you. The material covered here is a comprehensive starting point for your African spirituality journey and lays a good foundation for further research.

Chapter 3: Brujeria and Curanderismo

Brujeria and Curanderismo are two of the most misunderstood forms of folk magic. People often think of them as inherently evil or, in the case of Brujeria, simply another term for witchcraft. However, this isn't the case. In this chapter, we'll look at these practices in detail to understand what sets them apart from other folk magic traditions.

Brujeria and Curanderismo are two of the most misunderstood forms of folk magic.
https://www.pexels.com/photo/blindfolded-woman-with-a-candle-5435274/

Understanding Brujeria

Brujeria is the Spanish word for "witchcraft." However, it means more than simply witchcraft in another language. Instead, Brujeria is an indigenous system of folk magic with a long history, mainly practiced in Latin America and the Caribbean. The earliest known recording of this practice appeared in the 1500s. However, most brujas and brujos believe that the practice originates from the Aztec and Mayan civilizations of Mesoamerica.

As a result of slavery, Brujeria was forced to become a hidden practice. It was punished by Catholic land and enslavers who imposed their own views and beliefs. At the same time, transporting slaves around the Americas also led to the spread and development of Brujeria, as peoples from the continent came into contact with each other and shared their knowledge.

Although Brujeria is often denigrated as evil magic, in reality, it's the practice of magic – whether for good or evil. Brujas (female practitioners) and brujos (male practitioners) can practice both black and white magic. However, this depends on the individual practitioner and isn't a defining characteristic of Brujeria as a whole.

Gods in Brujeria

What sets Brujeria apart from many other folk magic traditions is the absence of a deity figure. Unlike many other indigenous practices like Santeria, Brujeria followers do not worship a particular god. Besides, contrary to most religious systems, there is no hierarchy of brujas and brujos.

It's essential to note that, due to the Catholicization of Latin America, Christianity is now deeply embedded in the practice of Brujeria. Many practitioners are also Christian, and many people hold Brujeria as a Christian system of folk magic. So, while Brujeria itself doesn't have any deity figure, this doesn't mean that practitioners do not worship a deity, and often, this deity is the Christian god.

Brujeria and Magic

As mentioned, brujas and brujos can be practitioners of both dark and light magic. They use a variety of magical techniques, including divination, spells, potions, herbalism, and more. When brujas and brujos are sought out for help, they usually prepare love potions, conduct divinatory magic, and perform charms and hexes.

As Brujeria flourished in parts of the world that were deeply Catholic, this led to a fear of Brujeria as being evil. At the same time, folk belief in brujas and brujos remained strong, and they were often sought out when all other solutions failed. This is especially true for healing rituals, as Brujeria practitioners are believed to both be able to inflict and heal curses caused by the "evil eye." So, when modern forms of healing have failed, Brujeria practitioners often seek to address curses that lie at the root of a person's illness.

Brujeria rituals are generally spontaneous and unplanned. Because no hierarchy exists in Brujeria, there are also no organized rituals. Each ritual that is performed is intensely personal to the practitioner. Similarly, building altars and summoning spirits is a personal experience that differs from one practitioner to the other. Due to the variety of spirits that can be called upon, it's challenging to imagine Brujeria ever becoming an institutionalized religion in the same way as Santeria.

Now, while rituals are a personal experience, brujas and brujos share certain similarities. Since Brujeria is not a standardized system of magic, it's an oral tradition of folk magic, and many oral Brujeria traditions share a similar origin. Many Brujeria practitioners also follow a number of other folk magic traditions, including Santeria and Vodou. They bring these belief systems to their practice of Brujeria, calling on Santeria Orishas and similar deities and entities, creating a hybrid magic tradition unique to them. They may also call on the recently deceased to help them with magic or to reveal secrets.

Some Brujeria practitioners, especially those who practice a combination of folk magic traditions, prefer not to be labeled as brujos and brujas but instead be called healers. For example, those who use energy magic may like to be called *energy healers*, while those using sound magic may prefer the title sound healers. Ultimately, each practitioner's preference is as personal as the practice of Brujeria itself.

While brujas and brujos may call on spirits, it is Brujeria practice never to question what is revealed to them by the spirits. It's believed that the spirits are merely there to show them what is meant to be shown, not to be questioned and forced to reveal secrets they aren't willing to reveal.

Modern Brujeria

Aside from magic and magic rituals, Brujeria practitioners also practice magic as a form of resistance. Many Brujeria practitioners see their magical tradition as a way of resisting colonization and reclaiming an indigenous practice that fell out of use due to pressure from the Catholic Church. For many practitioners, it served to reclaim an identity from which many had previously felt disconnected. This is especially true of Brujeria practitioners in the Latin American and Afro-Caribbean diaspora, who may not have the same connection to the land as native Latin American and Caribbean people.

At the same time, younger generations are starting to explore the world of Brujeria. This is because there are now far more brujas than brujos, and many women see Brujeria as a source of power that they may otherwise be lacking in a male-dominated world. Additionally, many people are becoming comfortable exploring family traditions, Brujeria, and magic. This is leading to more women becoming brujas, and it's once again common to find brujas and brujos in Latin American and Afro-Caribbean communities worldwide.

However, because Brujeria is an oral tradition, becoming a practitioner can be challenging. This is especially true if no one is there to instruct a new practitioner in their close family, as they must instead find an experienced guide in Brujeria.

Aside from rediscovering familial traditions of magic, what draws people to Brujeria is that it doesn't discriminate based on factors like age, ethnicity, or gender. While there are more brujas than brujos, this is simply a result of personal interest rather than oppression against male practitioners. Instead, Brujeria judges people on their abilities and the results they provide, making it a popular magical tradition for those looking to showcase and develop their powers.

Understanding Curanderismo

Curanderismo is a Latin American system of folk healing. It's found and practiced in many Latin American communities, including Mexico, Guatemala, Honduras, and Argentina. Curanderismo is often considered Mexican folk healing. However, this isn't the case. In Mexico, it's also known as "medicina del campo," or traditional folk medicine.

The history of Curanderismo is a long one. It traces back to various Mesoamerican civilizations, including the Olmecs, Aztecs, and Maya. It's essentially a combination and synthesis of several healing traditions found in these cultures, but other cultural and healing traditions and religions, including Roman Catholicism, have also influenced it.

As a result of cultural exchange and geographical proximity, Curanderismo also made its way to the United States. It was and remains most prominent in the country's southwest but is practiced nationwide. It was prevalent in indigenous communities, which had exchanges with Latin American peoples prior to Columbus' discovery in 1492.

Curanderas are healers who believe that disease is caused by a confluence of factors, not just physical or mental ones. Other influences can include environmental, spiritual, and social concerns. The goal of a curandera is to heal patients by helping them strike a balance between themselves and their surrounding environment.

There are many types of curanderas, depending on what type of healing they practice. Some include:

- Yerberos, or herbalists
- Hueseros, or bone and muscle healers
- Parteras, or midwives
- Oracionistas, or prayer healers
- Sobadors, or masseurs

In some practices, brujas and brujos may also be considered curanderas. This occurs when they use magic to treat illnesses of the soul or those caused by evil magic. In this position, they operate similarly to witch doctors.

Curanderismo is influenced by an amalgamation of different medical traditions. Aside from traditional Mesoamerican systems of healing, influences include African Santeria, the Greek theory of humor, Arabic healing traditions that help with the direction of psychic energy, and spiritualist traditions that help healers communicate with the spirits.

Curanderismo is also influenced by modern medical theories, such as germ theory. Many curanderas will advise patients with physical ailments to consult a modern allopathic doctor alongside their traditional treatment. This is because they believe modern medicine has its value and that curanderos don't have the answer to all ailments.

Gods in Curanderismo

Curanderismo can be considered a Catholic folk healing tradition to a certain extent. Many curanderas are Catholic and believe that the gift of healing is a gift from God. Several healing practices involve praying to God, and the training of curanderas involves prayer, religion, and learning to use both to help heal clients.

There is also the consideration that, for many curanderas, the decision to become a healer is less a conscious decision and more a "calling," similar to the calling to serve God in Catholicism. For that reason, the ability to practice Curanderismo is considered a healing gift from God.

Like in Brujeria, some curanderas bring other folk magic traditions to the practice of Curanderismo. This includes traditional Mesoamerican folk beliefs, African Santeria, and the belief in Orishas. Synthesis of these traditions creates a unique healing tradition for each curandera.

Curanderismo Healing

Curanderismo healing takes various forms, depending on the cause of the illness. Natural illnesses are treated with a combination of herbalism, prayer, and massage. However, even in the case of natural illnesses, curanderas work on all three levels the physical, spiritual, and mental. This involves:

- Treating the body with herbs, ritual healing practices, and conversation
- Treating the spirit with prayer and meditation. For some curanderas, this may also involve communication with spiritual beings like protectors, saints, and deities.
- Treating the mind with directional healing and mental focus

In Curanderismo, many illnesses are thought to be caused by intense emotions. These are "espanto" (scare), "bilis" (stress), and "susto" (fright). The event that caused the person to be startled typically involves a natural disaster, an accident, or a death in the family.

Some symptoms of susto are:
- Depression
- Insomnia
- Dreamless sleep

- Nervousness
- Diarrhea

Some symptoms of bilis are:
- Loss of appetite
- Irritability

Additionally, some illnesses are thought to be caused by mal aire or mal viento, meaning evil air or evil wind. These result from the movements of the air and can cause illnesses. Evil air can be hot or cold, and the illness can be caused by a movement from a hot space to a cooler space or vice versa.

Other causes of illnesses include dark Brujeria, when a curse is cast on a person, or when they encounter supernatural beings, including "espiritus" (spirits) and "duendes" (spirit creatures). Illnesses may also result from the "mal de ojo" (evil eye), an evil intent targeting a person, or a "mal projimo" (bad neighbor).

Lastly, there's also the case of soul loss. This may be the result of espanto or susto, or it may be an illness that affects a person independently of these ailments. Younger people are more prone to suffering from soul loss, and symptoms are similar to those experienced during susto and espanto.

Cases of physical and magical illnesses can be treated thanks to various "limpias," or purification rituals, in which specific objects and tools are used.

These can include:
- Eggs
- Holy water
- Herbs and spices
- Fruits (especially lemons)
- Flowers
- Incense
- Crystals
- Oils
- Pictures of saints
- Crucifixes and other religious objects
- Candles and incense

- Amulets
- Animal-based medicines (like snake oil and bufo toad medicine)

One of the best-known limpias is the temazcal ceremony, which is essentially the use of a sweat lodge. This ceremony is thought to remove impurities from a person's body and return them to the pure in-utero state.

Some limpias are relatively easy to perform and can be carried out by the individual rather than a curandera. By contrast, other limpias required a qualified practitioner to help lead the purification ceremony. Some limpias that you can perform on your own include:

Egg Cleanse

The egg cleanse is one of the most common limpias. It can be practiced by both professional brujas and curanderas, as well as individuals.

You'll need a fresh, clean, unmarked egg to perform an egg cleanse. The first step is to rinse it with a mix of salt water and lemon juice. If you are religious, you can reference the deity you follow while doing so (for example, Christians might make the sign of the cross over the egg or reference the Holy Trinity). When you have cleaned the egg, roll it over the part of your body that is hurt, injured, or aching. While doing so, ask the spirits to help heal your injuries by siphoning off the negative energy that's affecting your body into the egg.

After you've finished the healing portion of the limpia, the next step is to use the egg to divine your future. To do this, simply crack the egg open over a bowl and allow the yolk to fall out, discarding the white. Once the yolk has settled in the bowl, you can read it, similar to reading tea leaves. While this portion of the limpia is generally performed by an experienced curandera, there are some signs that are easily readable even by individuals. For example, a black yolk indicates bad luck and signifies that you should visit a bruja or curandera for more experienced help. Or, you can simply skip this step if you're not confident in your ability to read yolks.

Once the limpia is concluded, you can get rid of the egg and the negative energy it has absorbed by flushing all parts of it down the toilet. If you didn't use it to divine the future, you should first crack the egg before flushing it so that all the negative energy is released. After you flush it away, wash your toilet with salt and lemon juice to prevent any negative aura from lingering around your home.

Sweeping

This limpia is known as "barrida" in Spanish. You need three basic supplies for this one: a bundle of herbs, floral water, and a red string. Once you have the materials gathered, the first step is to bundle the herbs into a bouquet and tie them together with a portion of the red string. Wrap the remaining red string around your dominant hand (the one you write with). The red string should wrap around your palm at least twice so that it crisscrosses over the area.

Once it's ready, sprinkle floral water over the bouquet of herbs. If you're religious, you can also use holy water for this purpose. Stand up, holding the bundle of herbs that you just prepared, and focus on the intention of this limpia, which is to remove bad luck and negative energies from your body. You can also call on any deities, spirits, or gods you believe in while doing so. As you focus on your intentions, starting at the top of your head, use the bundle of herbs to "sweep" over your body.

The herbs sweeping over your body will eliminate all the negative energy from you. Once you're done with this step, dispose of the herbs in a bin outside your home. Remember to thoroughly clean your hands after you do so to clear away any lingering negative energies.

Some herbal medicines commonly used by curanderas as part of limpias include:

- Aloe vera
- Papaya
- Poultices
- Tobacco (for spiritual cleansing)
- Rosemary (for spiritual cleansing)

Curanderismo Today

Modern Curanderismo is practiced around the world, especially in Latin America and the United States. Several celebrity curanderas and curanderos are famous for their skills and abilities, such as Don Pedro Jaramillo, Teresa Urrea, and Niño Fidencio.

Modern curanderas also use social media to reach a new generation of people interested in traditional forms of healing. Because Curanderismo works in concert with modern medicine rather than against it, many people are willing to try it for chronic illnesses, particularly mental health issues.

Furthermore, Curanderismo is benefiting from the global popularity of alternative medicine. Several studies on the effects of Curanderismo are currently conducted, especially in treating mental health issues such as PTSD. Many traditional Curanderismo herbal medicines, such as aloe vera, are gaining popularity in modern medicine because of their curative properties.

Curanderas are easier than ever to find in Latin American communities worldwide. Many institutions offer Curanderismo training in Mexico and at the University of New Mexico.

Still, a great number of curanderas remain informally trained. Many traditional curanderas are trained in an oral tradition, from teacher to pupil. The institutionalization of Curanderismo is happening through formal training opportunities. However, it still remains incomplete, as many portions of the oral tradition of Curanderismo remain undocumented, existing only in the knowledge of individual practitioners.

Additionally, many traditional curanderas fear that Curanderismo is being appropriated and distorted by "curanderas" who do not know of the traditional practices. The conflict between these diverging forces will determine how Curanderismo is shaped and governed in the future.

Questions for Self-Reflection

Are you wondering if Curanderismo and Brujeria are the correct folk magic traditions for you to explore? If so, here are some questions you should ask yourself:

- Do I feel attracted to the traditions of Curanderismo and Brujeria?
- Do I have relatives in Latin America? Do I have Afro-Caribbean or Native American ancestors who may have learned and practiced these traditions?
- Do I feel drawn to heal other people?
- Have I ever experienced mal de ojo or mal aire? Have I felt these conditions in other people?
- Am I interested in personal forms of folk magic rather than systemized ones?
- Am I interested in attending a course that teaches Curanderismo?

Chapter 4: Scottish Witchcraft

According to the standard view, witchcraft is a type of magic where both male and female witches use supernatural powers to practice spells and charms for selfish or evil purposes. In medieval Europe, witches were hunted and persecuted, as witchcraft was regarded as a force for evil. For that reason, Scottish people couldn't use the terms witchcraft or witches as freely as they do today. In Scotland, a male witch was called "buidseach," and a female witch was called "bana-bhuidseach." These denominations were widely used during the 16th century when witches sought to protect their secret identities. Scottish witches at the time used magic and supernatural powers for self-gain, and their magic was often harmful to their community, which goes against what folk magic represents. Unless there was war, it was unwise for witches to practice evil magic as it turned their communities against them.

According to the common view, witchcraft is a type of magic where witches, both male, and female, use supernatural powers to practice spells and charms for selfish or evil purposes.

https://www.pexels.com/photo/an-old-book-and-candles-on-wooden-table-with-glass-bottles-7978061/

In Scottish folklore, the term *witch* is often associated with self-serving acts. They didn't help their community, which at the time was frowned upon as most people worked to help others and used their magic to provide services for their town folk. Scottish witchcraft included many types of practitioners, but the most significant ones were the wise men and women who were referred to as "bean/fear fease." While these individuals were considered witches, they never regarded themselves as such because their magic was a force for good rather than evil. Their community noticed what these folks were doing for them and understood their magic was different from that of witches. During the witchcraft trials in Scotland, the people asked the court to spare wise men and women. They held these wise folk in high regard because their magic wasn't self-serving. However, history has often been unkind to witches and anyone who practiced magic, forgetting that some good folk used their powers for good and in the service of others.

The wise folk in Scotland helped protect their communities against the forces of evil. In order to practice this type of magic, they had to be blessed by Daoine Sith, who were supernatural beings. Unlike other charmers or healers, these individuals were specialists who could communicate with a world beyond our physical one. The Daoine Sith bestowed wise men and women with a gift that enabled them to perform tasks that helped their communities. These tasks included predicting someone's death, finding lost or stolen objects, healing people from curses, and prescribing remedies for ailments.

The wise men and women were different from the cunning folks. Notably, charmers and healers didn't get their gift from the Sith, nor could they communicate with them, while the cunning folks got their knowledge from occult books. Scottish men and women who connected with the Sith could pass this gift to their children. Scottish clans also served as Sith helpers, making it easy to communicate with them and use their knowledge to practice magic.

History and Culture of Scottish Witchcraft

The history of Scottish witchcraft isn't pleasant, to say the least. Witches were essentially blamed for all the country's ills. People feared them, and as a result, the Scottish Parliament passed an act in 1563 that made witchcraft a capital offense. This act notably aimed to prevent the spread of pagan beliefs and the worship of saints and prohibit magic practitioners like the cunning folk from practicing. Witches struggled during these harsh times, not only because of the law but because people were hunting them as well. Moreover, healers and cunning folk were also the targets of this persecution. Cunning folk and healers were a force of good, using their magic to help the sick and protect them from evil spirits. It was a dark time in Scotland when all witchcraft practitioners were considered a danger, even those who helped their community.

Witches were blamed for any misfortune that occurred in the community. For example, in 1591, King James VI was at sea when a storm hit and almost sank his ship. About seventy witches were blamed for attempting to commit regicide. Any regular incident was considered a curse by witches, including when a child got sick or died prematurely, when crops didn't grow, or when cattle died. However, things changed in 1736 when the Parliament repealed the act, and witchcraft was no longer deemed a capital offense.

Nowadays, people still practice witchcraft in Scotland, and there aren't as many misconceptions about witches as before. People now know that images of witches flying on broomsticks or making spells over a cauldron are nothing but stereotypes. Most of the crimes witches were accused of back then weren't as serious as people made them out to be. In reality, many of these witches were helpful individuals who contributed to their communities.

Religion

Not much is known about religion in Scotland before the arrival of Christianity. However, historians believe its inhabitants were polytheists, like the Celts, who worshiped various deities and spirits. Pagans and the worship of deities influenced many branches of witchcraft. Scottish witchcraft is also syncretic, meaning it drew influences from several cultures and religions from all over the world, including Islam, Christianity, and Judaism.

Beliefs, Concepts, and Tradition

The Scottish people believed in supernatural beings and powers. These beliefs have been evident in Irish folklore for centuries. The Sith also had a great influence on Scottish witchcraft. "Sith" comes from the word Síd, whose various meanings include hill, goodwill, peace, and truce. These beings were believed to be fairies. Of note, various beliefs state that fairies are the spirits of the ancestors. The Scottish people believed that their ancestors lived in the otherworld. In fact, back then, they believed that the first person buried in a graveyard would later become its guardian. This is further proof that they believed the Sith were their dead ancestors.

Scottish practitioners communicated with the Sith to help with their magic. Some were clairvoyants, meaning they had the gift of second sight and could communicate with the other world. Those who didn't have this gift often used divination or made an offering. The Sith represented the dead that resided in the otherworld. Keeping a peaceful relationship with the Sith was essential to keeping the community safe. If one doesn't give them proper attention, they could inflict severe harm on local communities.

The fairy faith was also prominent among the common people. Some of their festivals, like Beltane (Bealltainn) and Samhain (Samhuinn), don't focus on worshiping a god or a goddess. Fairies have always been of the utmost significance, and these celebrations were focused on honoring their ancestors.

There are claims that some witches also believed in the devil, which was evident during the witches' trial in Scotland as some claimed to have renounced their baptism and made a deal with the devil. However, there are no records that prove witches worshiped the devil. It's believed that the church spread these rumors to scare people of witches and justify hunting them.

Scottish magic is also animistic and believes that everything, whether animate or inanimate, has a soul.

The people's belief system at the time focused on fairies, supernatural beings, spirits, the Devil, and religion.

Deities and Mythical Beings

Nicnevin

While the name Nicnevin may sound unfamiliar to most people, it's one that had a great impact on Scottish folklore and witchcraft. Nicnevin is a goddess and the queen of the fairies. Her name comes from Gaelic, meaning "daughter of frenzy." This etymology indicates that she could be linked to Neamhan, the Irish goddess of battle who made soldiers agitated during wars. Another theory, albeit not a very popular one, claims that Neamh means "heaven." It's also believed that this queen of the fairies comes from "Nic Noahm," which means "daughter of the Saint." While no one knows who this Saint may be, there are claims it was Saint Brigid.

Nicnevin's physical appearance isn't described in many literary works. However, in the few times her looks were mentioned, she was depicted as a woman wearing a long gray mantle. She also holds a powerful wand that gives her power over sea and land and allows her to alter her surroundings.

Nicnevin is also often compared to Cailleach – the goddess of winter and a prominent deity in Scottish and Irish mythology. Her name means "hag" or "the old woman." She is also known as Gyre-Carline – "Gyre" is Norse for greedy, and "Carline" is ancient Scottish that translates to "old woman." Another similarity between the two goddesses is that they rule over the sea and land and can transform their surroundings. Another theory regarding Nicnevin's origin that links her to Cailleach is that the "Nc" in her name means "the daughter of," while Nevis refers to Ben Nevis (mountain of snow). Ben Nevis is believed to be Cailleach's home.

Nicnevin is mentioned in various literary works and folklore. She was considered a scary figure that parents often used to scare children who misbehaved. She was also considered the queen of witches and a witch herself, which is why she is a prominent figure in Scottish witchcraft. Her first mention in Scottish literature was in a 16th-century poem by Alexander Montgomerie, where she appeared with her "nymphs," a term that describes female fairies. In the poem, we're told that she had charms, which refer to spells, implying that she was skilled in enchantment and divination. It also teaches us that she was riding with a fairy king, indicating that she may have been a fairy queen.

In Scotland, people consider Nicnevin a witch, even calling her "Grandmother Witch." During the witch trials, prosecutors often connected the witches to Nicnevin. Those who bore her name or a similar one were prosecuted. Various claims about Nicnevin linked her to Scottish witchcraft. Some say she was a regular human witch who was executed during the witch trials. Other claims attribute her to a more prominent role, namely, queen of witches.

Although much about Nicnevin is lost in history, all the information about her links her to fairies and witches. For that reason, Scottish witchcraft is inherently associated with the mythical figure of Nicnevin.

Cailleach

Also referred to as the "veiled one," Cailleach is the Celtic goddess of winter and winds and one of the oldest deities in Scottish mythology. Her name is a Scottish word that translates to "old woman." Cailleach is often depicted as an old woman wearing a veil and clothes decorated with skulls and having red teeth and pale skin. She had the ability to ride storms and shapeshift into an imposing bird. Considered both a destroyer and a creator, Cailleach was also referred to as the queen of the winter because she controlled its weather and duration. She was a significant figure in several countries in Europe as well.

Poets gave Cailleach various names in literary works and included her in several myths. She was called Buí, wife to Lugh, the god of justice, Biróg (who was a fairy), Digde, Burach, and Milucra. Due to her multiple names and the roles she played in mythology, scholars have debated whether Cailleach is a name or a title given to old women throughout history.

The old Gaelic "Cailleach phiseogach" means sorceress, and "Cailleach feasa" translates to *fortune teller*. For that reason, she is often referred to as a witch. Cailleach was a healer who used her ability to see into the future and cure the sick. She had knowledge of herbs, which she used to diagnose and treat many ailments, including emotional trauma. She would conduct her healing work to cure individuals and help heal entire communities.

In various stories, Cailleach is described as a woman wearing an apron and holding a wooden staff. In others, she is either holding a wand or a hammer. There are even other accounts of her holding a walking stick or a shillelagh. Invariably, whatever she was holding was made of the wood of a blackthorn tree, which has always been linked to witches and their powers. It's believed that the common depictions of witches as old women wearing black clothes and carrying a broom are influenced by the image of Cailleach.

Traits and Types of Scottish Witchcraft

Saining is a popular type of magic in Scottish culture, one with which many practitioners are familiar. It's an act of purification that resembles smudging but with slight differences. Practitioners would practice saining to get rid of negative spirits. It's usually done on people, animals, objects, and places. Since Scottish magic is animistic, the process of saining focuses on communicating with the spirit found inside each person and asking it to banish any negativity or evil spirits.

Various types of saining practices exist, each involving its own tool. The practice usually takes place in a community, over land, or around a specific person. Saining is most commonly conducted during festivals like Samhain and Beltane when people light huge fires to purify the entire town. Midwives would also purify newborns and their mothers. They do so by lighting a pine candle and spinning it around the bed three times while chanting a specific charm.

A characteristic trait of Scottish magic is its focus on healing spells and charms. When someone is ill, the wise man or woman would say a few words over the sick person and the water they were about to drink. This works on animals as well.

Another type of witchcraft involves granting protection for homes, animals, and people. To protect a person or animal from danger, the wise man or woman would utter a few healing words over the person's head, then place strings around their neck and leave them for a whole night. The wise folks would also tie a stone around a cow's tail while uttering a few words to protect them from evil.

For bacterial eye infections, the wise folk would leave the end of a stick in the fire, then take it out and point it at the infected eye. They would then spin the stick in circles while repeating a charm nine times.

Divinatory Practices

A few centuries ago, life was tough for Scottish Highlanders. As superstitious folk, witches, spirits, and fairies played a major role in their lives. Seeing as they blamed the witches for everything, any misfortune that would befall them was the witches' or fairies' fault. It was a time of uncertainty for the Scottish people. So, to protect themselves and their families, they turned to divination, often seeking the help of a seer or a person with second sight.

There are various types of divination practices, one of the oldest being speal bone divination. Practitioners would use an animal's shoulder blade after boiling it to foretell the future. They would also read tea leaves, one of the most popular divination practices in Scotland and around the world.

Many people prefer to practice divination on Samhain, which is the equivalent of modern Halloween. On Samhain, the veil between the world of the living and that of the dead is at its thinnest, meaning spirits and fairies can easily travel through it. Practitioners and wise folk would take advantage of this occasion to practice divination and seek advice and answers from the spirits. The festival of Beltane and Imbolc were also occasions for practicing divination. Scottish people believed no other days in the year were as powerful as the days of these festivals, which is why they presented the perfect opportunity to connect with the spirits and seek their wisdom.

Questions for Self-Reflection

- Do I have any Scottish ancestors?
- Have I ever had a dream of a Scottish deity or fairy?
- Do I agree with the beliefs of Scottish witchcraft?
- Do I feel attracted to Scottish witchcraft?
- How do I feel about the witch trials and how witches were treated back then?
- Do I want to learn more about Scottish witchcraft culture and history?
- What do I plan to do now with the information I have just learned?

Scottish witchcraft plays a prominent role in the world of magic. Although witches were persecuted and witchcraft was deemed a crime, many of the offenses they were accused of were unfounded. In reality, they were wise men, women, and cunning folk who helped their community and showed the world that magic could do more good than harm.

Chapter 5: Druidry and Celtic Magic

In the past few years, interest in spirituality has been on the rise. While many people have turned to Christianity or other well-established religions, others are exploring different ways of connecting with nature and finding peace within themselves. One of these paths is Celtic magic and Druidry. With over 7 million people identifying as Pagans, Heathens, Wiccans, or with other Neo-Pagan practices, the influence of these religions is growing worldwide. Druidry, in particular, is one such practice that has gained more attention recently. It's a religious tradition with ancient roots that has experienced a revival in recent years, particularly in Europe. Whether you're new to this faith and want to learn more about it or simply interested in exploring a new topic, this chapter will outline everything you need to know about Druidry and its followers today.

Druidry is a nature-based spiritual practice rooted in the ancient Indo-European culture that once spanned much of Europe and the British Isles.
https://www.pexels.com/photo/photo-of-the-stonehenge-historical-landmark-in-england-2497299/

Who Were the Druids?

The Druids were a group of people living in Europe and the British Isles thousands of years ago (3rd century BCE). According to historians, the Druidic religion was practiced in many parts of Europe, including Wales, Ireland, Scotland, France, and Spain. You can even find records of people practicing Druidry in modern times. The Druids studied and passed down knowledge about nature and natural laws. It's believed that they were also responsible for learning about ancient knowledge like language, culture, and philosophy. The Druids were also political leaders in Celtic societies. They're frequently featured in ancient historical accounts and folktales, which is why many people know about them today. They likely advised rulers on natural phenomena and served as judges. While there's no homogenous set of beliefs that all Druids follow, there are some common Druidic beliefs. One of these is a reverence for nature. Another is an interest in studying language, culture, and philosophy. Druids were also responsible for memorizing large amounts of lore, which they passed down orally.

The History of the Druids

Druidry is a nature-based spiritual practice rooted in the ancient Indo-European culture that once spanned much of Europe and the British Isles. The Druids were priests in the ancient Celtic society, where they studied and passed down lore about nature and natural laws. This likely included instructions for what we now call spirituality and philosophy. Many Druids were also political leaders in Celtic society, which is why they were largely featured in ancient historical accounts and folktales. Although historians disagree on how exactly Druidry and Celtic society operated, most agree that Druids were respected for their knowledge about the world, particularly the natural world.

There is very little historical evidence about the Druids and those who followed their beliefs. What is clear, however, is that the Druids were the religious leaders of the ancient Celtic people. The Druids held the world as a place of magic and mystery. According to them, all creation was alive with spirits and energies. The Druids followed a path of nature worship, meaning they revered and honored the beauty and power of nature. The Druids believed that all natural things had spirits or "souls," just like humans. They also had a deep and powerful connection to the creative energy of nature, which they called "the Force," and they believed that it flowed through all things, even rocks, trees, and plants. This creative energy was also present in humans. The Druids believed that everyone had the ability to harness and channel this creative force.

Druid Influences

Many people who practice Druidry today blend it with other magical or religious paths. Druidry has Celtic roots, but there are many other influences as well. These include:

- **Wicca and Witchcraft:** The most common path people blend Druidry with is Wicca or Witchcraft. Both of these paths include a belief in the power of the Force and a practice of channeling and working with it.
- **Magical herbs:** Celtic druids were also known for their knowledge of the magical herbs and plants found on their land. These herbs were thought to hold special powers and energies that could be used in various spells and rituals.
- **The elements:** Druidry is also often blended with the practice of working with the "elements." This belief holds that the natural world comprises four elements: fire, water, earth, and air.

Beliefs and Concepts

Like many other faiths, there isn't a single "Druid belief" or set of beliefs to which all Druids adhere. While they tend to share certain views, Druids interpret these ideas in different ways. The most commonly shared Druid belief is a reverence for nature. Druids believe that all of nature is sacred and interconnected in a web of life, including humans.

The Druids believed that everything in nature has a soul or spirit, including rocks, trees, plants, rivers, and lakes. There are no "ordinary" or "mundane" things or creatures in the world. To them, all is sacred and magical. Everything is connected and interdependent. The trees are connected to the mountains, the mountains are connected to the rivers, and so on. Everything is also connected to humans. It is our job to "listen" to nature and learn from it. The Druids believed that everything in the world holds a special creative energy, and anyone who is willing has the ability to channel and harness this force.

The Druids used this creative energy in their healing, spells, and in their everyday lives. One of the most important tools for Druids was the wheel of the year, a calendar that marks important holy days in the year. The wheel of the year is split into 8 seasons, with each season lasting about two months. The seasons of the year are related to the cycle of nature and the plants growing and dying.

Key Practices of Druidism

Druids believe that nature is full of magic. It's a basic belief in Druidry that everything in nature is magical and that each person can access this magic through their connection to nature. For that reason, many Druids refer to their spiritual practice as "sorcery" instead of "magic." Druids practice a form of magic based on their connection to nature. They use plants, herbs, crystals, and other natural elements to connect with the spirits of the natural world. The Druidic concept of magic is based on the world as a living, breathing thing instead of a lifeless, impersonal machine. Rather than a mechanical system of cause and effect, it's a creative process that is constantly transforming and evolving. Druids believe everything is connected and the entire world is one organism. This allowed them to leverage the power of plants, animals, stones, and other natural elements to create magic that helped them achieve their spiritual goals.

Who Can Practice Druidry?

Anyone can practice Celtic magic and Druidry, regardless of age, gender, or religion. In fact, this path has been followed by people from all walks of life for millennia. It's a great way to connect with nature, find peace and order in your life, and learn more about yourself in the process. If you want to learn about Celtic magic and Druidry in greater detail, you'll find plenty of dedicated articles and books on the topic. Finding others who are interested in this particular path will also help you grow your knowledge, share ideas, and practice together.

The Ancient and Magical Art of Druidism: What Did Druids Use for Divination and Spells?

Delving a little deeper into the world of druids and their practices, you'll discover a lot more fascinating things about this mysterious group. They were a highly respected group with many followers. Today, many people follow the ancient ways of the Druids and incorporate their practices into daily life. The spells, rituals, and beliefs are not exclusive to any group but can be found across several cultures worldwide.

Much of what we know about the Druids has come from the writings of Roman and Greek historians, who weren't exactly unbiased sources. These accounts, which describe the Druids as a mysterious order of priests and natural philosophers, are filled with exaggerations and half-truths. A complete picture of what life was like for pre-Christian Celtic people is still unclear. However, there are things we do know for certain. The Celts believed in many spirits that inhabited their world. They had several gods and goddesses, each with their own strengths and weaknesses. And like many other folks, they practiced this magical art through spells and divination methods.

Druid Divination Tools and Practices

Before we delve into Druid spells and divination practices, it's helpful to understand the core beliefs that governed Celtic magical practices. First and foremost, people back in the Iron Age (the period in which the Celts lived) believed that everything in the world contained some kind of spirit. In Gaelic, these spirits were called "sidh." A sidh could inhabit anything - plants, trees, lakes, rocks, and even minerals. The Celts often placed offerings at these spots or asked the sidh for guidance. In parallel, the Celts used various divination methods to communicate with the spirits. Perhaps the most common way was through the use of augury (reading omens). They would observe nature and interpret what the spirits were telling them through the movement of birds and flight of insects, the motion of water, or the entrails of animals.

Druid Rituals and Ceremonies

Traditionally, Druids also performed rituals and ceremonies with the goal of influencing the world. One of the most common rituals was called "mutation," whose intent was to transform one thing into another. An example of a mutation ritual is the transformation of a caterpillar into a butterfly. Over time, the practicing Druid would watch the caterpillar carefully as it transformed into a butterfly. After careful observation, they would try to imitate the caterpillar's transformation in their ritual. This ritual was designed to transfer the butterfly's powers to the Druid. Another common ritual was called "immolation." This ritual was a form of sacrifice, often involving the killing or burning of animals. Immolation rituals were performed to appease the gods. If the Celts wanted rain or a bountiful harvest, they would conduct a rain or harvest ritual. If there was a plague or disease, they would perform a ritual to appease the gods and ask them to lift the plague.

Divination and Spells

While it's impossible to know precisely what kinds of spells the Druids used, we can make some educated guesses based on ancient stories. One of the most well-known accounts from the Celtic tradition is that of the Salmon of Knowledge. In this story, a young man named Finn McCool is tasked with finding wisdom and knowledge. As part of this journey, he set off to find a salmon that would leap out of a pool, eat his thumb, and then die. Finn waited for hours for the salmon to jump out. Then, suddenly, a salmon leaped out and ate his thumb. He hurried back to the pool, caught the salmon, and put it on a rock to die. When the young man returned to the rock to retrieve the dead salmon, he found it had turned into an old man. The old man revealed he was an ancient Druid who'd been trapped in the salmon's body for many years. The Salmon of Knowledge was one of the most popular spells used by the Druids.

Gods and Goddesses

A shared characteristic of ancient cultures is that they had a pantheon of gods and goddesses, and the Celts were no exception. While the Celts believed in many gods, two were more prominent than others. The first was Lug (Lugh), the god of the sun. He was associated with the harvest and growing season and was said to be a god of poetry and inspiration. The other prominent deity was Nemain, the goddess of war and death. Nemain was known for her fury in battle. She was particularly important to the Gauls, the Celtic people who fought against the Romans.

Basics of Druid Magic and Divination Today

No single definition could pay proper justice to the Druids' magic and divination methods. Each person who practices these arts adopts the Druidic way of life in their own personal way. Since Druid magic is rooted in nature and draws its power from the earth, the practice is inherently connected to the environment, taking inspiration from the elements of nature. Druids believed everything in nature held a connection with the universe and the divine. They used their surroundings to enhance their Druidic spells and castings by finding materials found nearby. For example, they would use natural items with healing properties, such as coneflowers and lavender, to cast a spell for healing.

Modern Druidry

Unfortunately, there's no detailed guidebook on how to become a Druid. You must decide to walk this path and follow the guidance of your inner Druid. It may take a few years, or even longer, before you fully understand your Druid path. By remaining faithful and practicing, you'll eventually get there.

It's important to note that many different branches of Druidism exist, although most of them have more in common than not. Still, there are variations in practices and interpretations of Druid beliefs. The types of Druidism range from ancient Druid groups such as the Order of Bards, Ovates, and Druids (OBOD), the Ancient Order of Druids (AOD), to Neo-Druidism practice such as Hedge Druids (those who practice alone) and Grove Druids (those who practice within a small group).

Hedge Druids

Hedge Druids essentially combine Druidry and witchcraft. This term often refers to people outside of traditional lines of power and knowledge. They focus on balancing the elements, using nature to help achieve goals. They seek to connect with their environment, commune with spirits, and use their power for good. Here, the word "hedge" refers to the way they combine traditional magic and herbalism with modern environmentalism. They believe our relationship with the natural world is key to bringing about positive change in our lives. Without it, we risk falling prey to negative influences. A hedge Druid seeks balance between mind, body, spirit, and environment, working together as a whole system. This means they are open to all forms of wisdom, no matter where it comes from – whether it's spiritual or scientific. Ultimately, they hope to create harmony between humans and the Earth by learning how best to care for both.

Druid's Grove

A Druid grove is a small group of people who come together to celebrate and explore ancient Celtic spirituality and Druidism. It's a place where they connect with the natural world and each other. There are many benefits to joining a Druid grove, including meeting new and interesting people, learning more about Celtic culture and spirituality, and having a place to explore and grow as an individual. Luckily, you don't need to be an expert or have a lot of experience to join Druid grove. Many groves and groups are dedicated to newcomers, providing a safe place to ask questions. If you're interested in Druidism, you can find a group in your area or online. Ultimately, Druidism can be a great way to connect with nature, gain a deeper understanding of the world, and feel more fulfilled.

Is Druidry and Celtic Magic for You?

Druids are often viewed as nature lovers who practice a religion deeply rooted in the beauty and harmony of nature. While that is certainly true, the Druid tradition isn't limited to a love of nature. Druids are spiritual seekers who strive to connect with the natural world and with their own inner wisdom. They're also open to new ideas and ways of thinking. Druidism can be a great choice for people who want to learn about spirituality but aren't sure where to start or those who need guidance along the way. It may also be a good fit for people who feel disconnected from the surrounding world and wish to reconnect with nature. Druidism can help connect you with your own natural emotional state, so you can better understand yourself and others. This can be a powerful way to improve your relationships, increase self-awareness, and build confidence.

Due to the connection with nature, many people find Druidry and Celtic magic to be good alternatives for people to connect with the Earth and its natural cycles. Ask yourself the following questions to help you

decide whether this practice is for you:
- Do I have an interest in plants, animals, or the earth itself?
- Do I feel connected to or concerned about the environment?
- Do I want to develop my intuition and awareness?
- Do I want to build a sense of spirituality?

Am I interested in the traditions and cultures of ancient belief systems?

In ancient cultures, druids were a privileged class of people who practiced the arts of nature and spirituality. These mystical men and women had extensive knowledge of the natural world, which they used in their rituals and practices. With their intimate connection to nature, Druids used various spells and divination methods to manipulate natural elements. From these practices, we can learn essential skills that can help us live happier, more fulfilled lives.

Chapter 6: Norse Paganism

The world's diversity of religious traditions is fascinating. Many of these faith systems have existed for thousands of years, and many continue to be practiced today. Some are well known, whereas others don't enjoy the same popularity. Each religion provides its followers with an insight into the world and our place in it. Even though Christianity is currently the largest religion in the world, other belief systems have been around for just as long, and even longer, although they don't receive as much attention as they once did. One such religious tradition is the Norse Paganism faith system.

Each religion provides its followers with an insight into the world and our place in it.
https://www.pexels.com/photo/a-person-covering-the-lighted-candle-he-is-holding-5435272/

Many people are intrigued by Norse Paganism but aren't exactly sure what it is or how it differs from other belief systems like Wicca or Druidism. In this chapter, we will explore everything you need to know about this lesser-known Scandinavian faith system, including what it is, its history, key practices, and famous figures.

What Is Norse Paganism?

Norse Paganism is an ancient religious faith system practiced by the Northern Germanic and Anglo-Saxons during the Viking Age (approximately 800-1100 CE). Norse paganism is sometimes referred to as Heathenism. The religion is based on an animistic worldview in which the universe is a giant organism where all creatures, planets, and even objects have souls. Norse pagans believe in a divine force known as the "Wyrd" or "Fate," which guides the universe and controls the fates of all beings.

The Norse were a Northern Germanic people who inhabited modern-day Scandinavia (Denmark, Norway, Sweden, Finland, and Iceland) during the Viking Age. Unfortunately, much of their history has been lost over time. Most of our current knowledge about the Norse tribes comes from a time after they converted to Christianity. While the details of Norse Paganism are not entirely clear, we do know that it's based on a pantheon of deities called the Aesir and Vanir. They include gods and goddesses, each representing different powers and characteristics to call upon during difficult times or for worship to give thanks. Some of the more prominent deities in Norse paganism include Odin, Freyr, Frigg, Thor, and Tyr.

The Norse Subgroup Asatru

The Norse people once thrived throughout much of Northern Europe and are known for their love of battle, bravery, and strong thirst for drinking. These brave, strong people had a culture so rich in tradition that it has survived to the present day, not just as fragments or antiquated stories but as an active religion with followers all over the world.

Asatru is the subgroup of Norse paganism followed by most contemporary practitioners of the religion. Asatru literally translates to "belief in the gods." It's an umbrella term that refers to many different types of Germanic paganism. Asatru began to emerge in the 20th century in reaction to the increasing influence of Christianity in Northern Europe.

The first Asatru group was founded in the 1970s. Today, Asatru is a recognized religion in several countries, with over 4,000 members in Iceland alone. While Asatru followers are largely united by their reverence for the Norse gods, certain other aspects of the religion are subject to debate. Some Asatru groups have adopted ideas from other Germanic pagan traditions, while others have remained faithful to the original Norse religion.

The History of Norse Paganism

Much of what we know about the early Norse faith comes from archaeological evidence, artifacts, and extant literature. As already mentioned, much of the information and practices of Norse Paganism were lost due to the conversion of the Norse people to Christianity. However, we do know that the Norse tribes were polytheistic, meaning that they believed in multiple deities. There are written sources regarding Norse Paganism dating back to the 10th century. These texts show that the Norse tribes were already converting to Christianity at this time and that Christianity was already widely practiced among the Norse people. Norse Paganism likely began to decline after the 11th century, and many of the Norse tribes likely converted to Christianity completely by the 12th or 13th century.

While there's a great deal of debate over the origins of the Norse people, the most widely accepted theory is that they migrated to Northern Europe from Southeastern Russia. The Norse were seafaring people who built large wooden longboats, called Viking ships, which enabled them to travel vast distances and establish settlements in areas such as Greenland, Canada, and even parts of Northern Africa. The Norse were also skilled craftsmen who produced beautiful artwork and intricate jewelry out of silver and gold. The Norse adhered to an animistic religion known as Norse Paganism. This religion was based on the belief that the universe was an organic organism that was created and sustained by a divine power known as the Wyrd. The Norse believed that every person, animal, and even inanimate objects, like trees, had souls.

Norse Pagan Influences

While Norse paganism is an ancient religion, it's also an evolving faith that has been shaped by the cultures of the different peoples that have practiced it. For example, Viking explorers traveled as far as Greenland

and North America, bringing Norse paganism with them. However, the Inuit people they encountered were so different from the Norse people that they quickly incorporated Inuit customs into the Norse faith. Similarly, Norse pagans who migrated to Anglo-Saxon regions like England and Scotland had to adapt their rituals and practices to suit the cultures they encountered in those places. Therefore, the Norse religion has greatly evolved over time, taking on new customs, rituals, and traditions.

Norse Pagan Beliefs

While there's no one definition of paganism, it can be broadly defined as a set of beliefs and practices centered around nature and the elements. At its core, paganism is a worldview that emphasizes the interconnectedness between all things. It views nature as a source of inspiration and wisdom and seeks to honor and care for it. This worldview is also often rooted in reverence for the supreme being(s) and that all creatures, including humans, will be reincarnated after death if the gods are properly honored.

Norse beliefs fall into either one of two groups - those that arose from the old religion and those that evolved from the Christianization of Scandinavia. The latter group takes the form of folkloric stories, whereas the first group is manifested through archaeological findings and artifacts. Both sets of beliefs attempt to answer several questions about life, death, and rebirth. This includes existentialist considerations, such as why there is suffering in the world, but also deals with more transcendent ideas, such as fate, predestination, and free will. How did we get here? Where did we come from? How did we end up on this planet? These are some of the most important questions we must answer in order to find meaning in life. We must understand our origin story to know where we came from. In that regard, Norse mythology provides an excellent basis to answer these questions.

Key Practices of Norse Paganism

There are various practices associated with Norse Paganism. While many of them are difficult to decipher due to the loss of records, we do know of certain rituals and observances associated with this faith system. The Norse had a unique set of beliefs that involved magic, runes, gods, and other mythological creatures. They also had complex rituals and ceremonies centered on death, rebirth, and nature. For example, some written records indicate that the Norse people performed human sacrifices as part of the worship of the deities. Many Norse Pagans also participated in seidr, which is a form of shamanic magic. In seidr, practitioners enter a trance-like state in order to connect with the spiritual realm, communicate with deities, and practice healing. There are also written accounts mentioning that the Norse people engaged in blót, a ritual of sacrifice and feasting in honor of the deities.

Why Should We Care about Norse Paganism?

Norse Paganism is a fascinating religion that offers a unique perspective on the world. This religious tradition is a reminder that there are different belief systems that are just as old as Christianity but don't receive as much attention. Norse Paganism is particularly important because it offers a glimpse into what our world was like before the rise of Christianity. It's a way for us to gain insight into how other people perceive the world and their place in it. Norse Paganism is also significant because it shows how difficult it would have been for people to convert to Christianity. The Norse people were dedicated to their religion, and it took centuries for Christianity to gain a foothold in Northern Europe.

The Norse Druids and Magic

The Norse are renowned for their daring raids and fearless exploration of new lands. Their traditions thrived in the harsh climate of Northern Europe, and they developed a strong sense of faith in the gods, who they believed watched over them at all times. They believed the natural world was full of magic and that certain people were blessed with special powers known as "visions." These druids, or "see-ers" as they were known, played an important part in Norse society and assisted the chieftain with his duties and provided advice on important decisions. The druids also used their magical powers to aid the warriors before battle.

They were a sophisticated and complex culture, with great variety from region to region. They had rich traditions, many of which we still don't fully understand today. Norse druids and magical runes are just one example. It's well-known that the Vikings had a deep respect for nature and its many wonders, as evidenced by their frequent expeditions into the wilderness for hunting and fishing. However, some of the Vikings' practices appear to be more than mere reverence toward nature. In fact, several accounts of rituals seem to have been based on magic, particularly involving the use of special words (or "runes") as a way to connect with the spirit world or harness divine energy. Let's explore these curious accounts and attempt to understand what they could have meant in practice.

Norse Runes

Runes are an alphabet used by many cultures throughout Northern Europe, including the Vikings. The German word "runen" actually means "mystery" or "secret," highlighting how mysterious these alphabets seemed to people, and still do, even today. Although the origin and development of runes are still largely unknown, we know they were used for various purposes. Most commonly, runes were carved onto stones as a form of writing. Other materials like wood and metal were also used for inscriptions. However, there's also evidence that runes were used for other purposes, such as magic, divination, and even healing.

Many great cultures have used runes for divination. Among them are the Anglo-Saxons, Celts, and even the Vikings. In fact, the tradition of using runes for divination is so strong that runes have become synonymous with fortune-telling in many modern languages.

Norse Pagan Magic

The term "Paganism" broadly describes a wide range of diverse religions and philosophies. It's typically used as an umbrella term to encompass modern Neopaganism and Wiccan religions but can also be used to refer to pre-Christian cultures such as the Celtic, Germanic, Slavic, or South Asian peoples. The definition of "Pagan" varies widely according to individuals and groups. Many Neopagans self-identify as Pagan by default, whereas others may not identify with any particular religion. Neopagans who identify as Pagan tend to be more interested in their spiritual side than in any particular set of practices or rituals. These people may engage in one or more of the following practices: meditation, yoga, natural medicine, divination (including tarot reading and runes), nature-based spirituality, or other types of spiritual practices.

There is a staggering number of books and videos on the subject of Pagan magic. However, as you explore this fascinating topic, several things must be kept in mind. Firstly, Pagan magic is not synonymous with Wicca. While Wicca is a specific type of modern witchcraft that incorporates elements from nature worship and Celtic spirituality, Pagan magic is simply any form of magic that originates outside mainstream Christianity. Secondly, Pagan magic does not necessarily have to be white-washed. Many forms of Pagan magic out there incorporate certain aspects of

African, Asian, Native American, or other cultures. Thirdly, while Norse magic can take many different forms, it all traces back to one core belief, the power of the individual to control their own destiny. By tapping into this power, you can harness the full potential of your body, mind, and spirit for positive change.

Norse Pagan Rituals and Ceremonies

Most of the evidence for Norse Paganism comes from archeological finds. Most of these items are what we call votive offerings, which are things that people would leave behind to show respect to a deity or ask for a favor. These range from small pieces of jewelry to larger items like furniture or statues.

There is also a lot of evidence in written sources. There is no consensus of opinion among scholars on when and how the religion was practiced, but there are a few things that seem to be consistent across all sources. Firstly, there are references to rituals that were used to honor specific deities and ask for their help. Secondly, there are references to runes and other magical symbols. Thirdly, there is a lot of talk about spirits that appear in dreams and other forms of communication with the spirit world.

Other types of evidence, mainly from ancient texts, suggest that Norse rituals involved casting spells for healing or protection, making offerings to gods and goddesses, or creating sacred spaces for the ceremony. Sacrifices were also common in Norse paganism. Sacrifices, called "blót," could take many forms, including offerings of food and drink, animal sacrifices, burning incense or candles, and setting an object on fire. The type of sacrifice depended on the purpose of the ritual. For example, if you want to heal someone, you might sacrifice food or drink to help nourish their body.

In Honor of the Gods and Goddesses

Several accounts describe rituals involving specific gods or goddesses. For example, there are reports that Vikings would perform a ritual before traveling at sea to honor the god Tyr and ask for his protection. Similarly, there's a story about a Viking who became sick and was advised to sacrifice to the god Frey to be healed.

There are several explanations for why Vikings performed rituals and used runes for magic. Some scholars suggest that they were simply trying to mimic what they believed the gods themselves had done. Others argue that they were attempting to influence their gods and draw their power. Finally, some claim that these rituals were designed to create a sense of community and comfort and connect people with each other.

How to Practice Norse Paganism

If you're intrigued by Norse Paganism and want to learn more about this ancient faith system, you can do a few things. First, you can read up on the Aesir deities and explore their stories. It's best to read secondary sources like books or online articles, as Viking-age texts are often complex and difficult to interpret. Second, you can explore the writings of modern practitioners of Norse Paganism to gain insight into how people practice the faith today. Finally, you can explore the archaeological evidence and other artifacts associated with the Norse people. This may help you better understand the people and the faith system. So, if you're interested in Norse Paganism, there's no time like the present to learn more about this fascinating religion.

Is Norse Paganism for You?

While some people are actively trying to revive ancient Pagan traditions and practices in today's world, for most people, this term is simply a catchall for any interest in religion or spirituality that isn't explicitly tied to Christianity. If you're unsure what you believe or looking for an inclusive, personal spiritual path, consider Norse paganism. There are many paths you can take, from the simplest forms of nature worship and gratitude practice all the way up to more complex ideas about the relationship between humans and their surroundings. As long as you respect your vision and work respectfully with others, you don't need to feel pressured to fit into a single mold. Ask yourself the following questions to help you decide if this practice is the right one for you:

- Am I looking for an inclusive faith system?
- Do I feel attracted to the concept of the runes?
- Do I want the freedom to choose which parts of the faith to practice?
- Am I willing to learn about the various gods and goddesses within this faith?
- Do I prefer the idea of spirituality over a specific religion?
- Am I interested in meditation and self-reflection?

- Does the idea of deity veneration appeal to me?

As you can see, the Norse were a complex people with a rich history and culture. However, we are only just beginning to understand them, and there's still much to learn about this fascinating civilization. As modern-day archaeologists keep digging up new discoveries, we are gaining new insights into the Vikings' history, culture, religion, and practices. Norse druids and magical runes are just one example of the many complex traditions that the Vikings had. Keep in mind, though, that Norse paganism is an ancient religion that has evolved over time. While these facts provide a solid foundation, they're not the last word on Norse paganism. As religion continues to change, new ideas will inform and enrich the faith, making it even stronger.

Chapter 7: Jewish Magic and the Kabbalah

With its diverse forms, Jewish mysticism is one of the most multifaceted religious traditions worldwide. The practice varies from moderate intellectual pursuits of understanding the Creator's world to intensive experimentation in non-religious activities. The former incorporates the traditional aspects of Judaism, including following the commandments of the Torah. While this form typically infuses Torah practices with mystical symbolism, the experimentative side relies on grounding activities to communicate with the Creator. Reading this chapter, you'll see how Kabbalah, the most widely known form of Jewish mysticism, combines both practices. You'll also discover how the traditional elements meet the mystical side in the Tree of Life and the Sefirot.

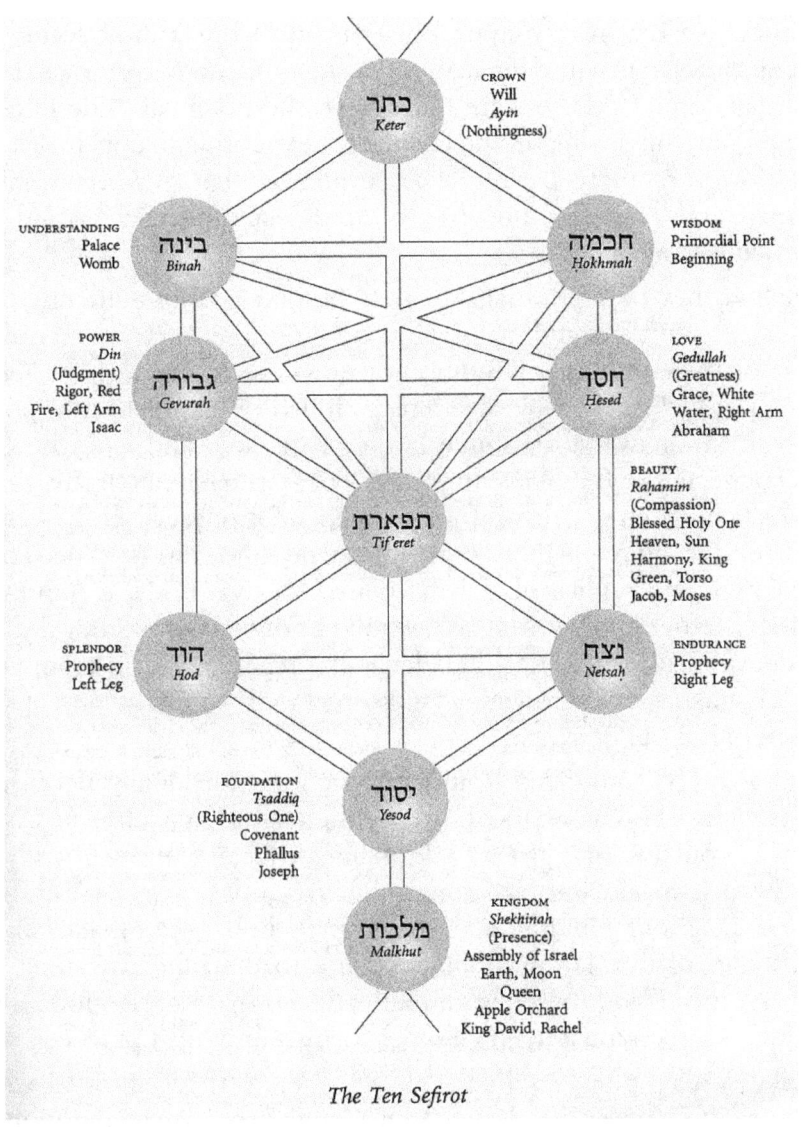

Jewish mysticism is one of the most multifaceted religious traditions worldwide.
Edaina, CC BY-SA 3.0 <http://creativecommons.org/licenses/by-sa/3.0/>, via Wikimedia Commons: https://commons.wikimedia.org/wiki/File:The_one_tr%C3%A4d.jpg

What Defines Jewish Magic?

Traditional Jewish mysticism represents a collection of practices designed to reach the divine source presented by the Torah. Because of this, this sacred book is considered the pillar for authentic Jewish mysticism – and by extension, Jewish magic. Records of magical and supernatural experiences, such as receiving prophecies and visions, can be found in the works of various mystics throughout history. Certain historical records suggest that some of these were considered the potential "side effects" of the life of a mystic dealing in the occult and experimenting with folk magic tools. However, there's also clear evidence that Jewish magic was performed only for the purpose of understanding the natural order established by the Creator.

Whether they perform magic or not, the only goal of authentic mystics is to seek the understanding of God and his presence in nature. The purpose of their practices is unification with the essence of the Creator. This is typically achieved by obtaining as much of his wisdom as possible. They seek to uncover the infinite layers of the soul and learn how one's soul is connected to the heavenly spheres of spirituality. Not only that, but their practices often go beyond the concept of a physical body - or even behind the teachings of the Torah related to one's body. The Torah is often viewed as a replica of a living being. It has a body, a mind, and a soul, tied together and working as a whole. For that reason, they are always dependent on each other. An imbalance in one creates disharmony in the entire organism. The universe is also viewed similarly, just like the organism of human beings.

Neither body, mind, nor soul can function individually because they aren't isolated. Likewise, the body of the Torah (nigleh) can't survive without its soul (nistar), just as a human body can't function without its soul. Through magic and traditional practices, mystics seek to unite their body and their soul - and all the esoteric parts in between (halacha) - with the teachings of the Torah. This exposure to the inner meaning of the Torah and the divine forces within all of us is what defines Jewish magic and mystics, separating it from all other forms of mystical practices.

Unlike similar practices that seek a higher form of spiritual wisdom, Jewish magic is never used to confirm any preconceived notion. The answers mystics are known to pursue only serve to reveal the divine truth, even if it's different from what they were aware of. Mystics throughout history have used magic to discover what motivates human souls and what helps them grow spiritually. Those who reached an elevated state could glimpse the genuine and divine reality of the Creator - and their insights were verifiable. In fact, many of these insights are still being tested and proven today through modern Jewish magical practices.

Kabbalah and Jewish Magic

Kabbalah is the oldest and most notorious form of Jewish mysticism. Its roots are based on the writing of the Zohar, a collection of spiritual teachings and Jewish magical practices uncovered around the Middle Ages, originally written around the 2nd century. The English name of the Kabbalah stems from the word "cabal," meaning a "secret group" or "conspiracy," and was first used by medieval Christian writers. The same writers, rather than trying to fully understand the practices they were describing, made them forcefully fit into the doctrines of their own religion. As a result, there are still many misunderstandings surrounding Jewish mysticism, Kabbalah, and Jewish magic.

After its re-discovery around the 13th century, Kabbalah began to rise in popularity due to its connection to the Torah. It also contains a thorough description of the Sefirot, the only form of divine quality known to people. The revelation of this essence is a way to provide people with a better understanding of how the creation took place. After the 16th century, mystics began to delve into the experimental side of Kabbalah, combining its teachings with folk magic practices. This gave birth to a new form of Kabbalistic approach known today as contemporary Jewish magic.

Kabbalah means "tradition," signifying that Jewish magic tends to rely on conventional Jewish values and teachings. Due to this, it can't simply be a collection of personal insights and wisdom gained through mystical experiences. It's not even a system of magical practices practitioners developed due to their own cultural and religious backgrounds. It's a little bit of both. It also incorporates the elements of cosmology, ontology, and cosmology. As mentioned before, Kabbalah is based on the revelation of the Torah, not on speculative theories developed by people trying to find reasons for divine occurrences. It seeks to explore the relationship between the divine and its creations.

Mystics who delved into magic realized that the best way to test the hypothesis of Kabbalah is by experiencing them through magical practices. They considered the theories and prospective experiences, tested them, and after they managed to verify them, they labeled them as acceptable. Many of these mystics have immortalized their findings, providing reliable sources for working on the different aspects (essences), allowing future generations to continue these practices.

The Hebrew records of Kabbalistic practices also interpret the meaning of Kabbalah as "to receive and accept" and "tradition," yet another reason this school of thought became so popular. By accepting old traditions and combining them with Kaballalstic Jewish magic, they can better understand the divine as well as themselves.

The Tree of Life and the Archangels

According to Kabbalah, the Creator's energy cannot be portrayed in its elementary form because it is incomparable to anything humans will ever experience. The true essence of the Creator, known as "Ein Sof," has no boundaries and transcends everything and everyone. People and the universe itself interact with different energies by finding a point within a particular power that aligns with their energies. Ein Sof literally translates as "without end." This means this energy doesn't have an end or beginning people can grab onto and align themselves with. And this is why no one can interact with it directly. The sacred qualities, however, can be portrayed through their interaction with the universe through its offspring, the divine creations. The most famous illustration of the divine essence is the Ten Sefirot. The Sefirot also expresses how the Creator communicates with people – by showering his creative energy into the universe, which is picked up by the angels and further distributed to people. The interaction is exemplified in The Tree of Life, which has ten branches. Each branch represents a Sefirot, a form of the divine essence, and an Archangel that oversees the distribution of powers. The Archangels are beings born on the first day of creation and have since accumulated immense wisdom. For that reason, each of them has acquired a unique specialty. Their specialties are linked to the part of the divine essence they are charged to oversee. According to the Sefer Yetzirah (the Jewish book of creation), the Archangels are associated with the four natural elements of fire, water, air, and earth, as well as with the four divine elements, dominion, strength, mercy, and beauty.

The Tree of Life, also known as the flower or seed of life, has a female and a male side. The male energy is carried on the right side through the sephirah of wisdom, crown, eternity, kindness, and beauty. Whereas the female energy travels through the left side, enveloping the sephirah of splendor, understanding, kingship, foundation, and severity. The tree has a section called the "head," which contains the Sefirots' understanding, crown, and wisdom, all with the capacity to distribute the divine essence to the lower branches. These, in turn, are called the "body," and they illuminate the practical and emotional side of the divine.

While they often manifest themselves in human form, some claim that angels may also appear as spirits. Presumably, this is because people who experience interactions with them in the spiritual form are usually able to perceive only their spiritual energy and not their visual form. According to Kabbalah, angels live in a spiritual space where they can absorb the divine essence. This area is found between two of the Kabbalah worlds, Yetzirah (formation) and Beriah (creation). After delivering the divine message down below, angels help people elevate their energies into higher spiritual planes. Below, you'll see how each Sefirot is linked to the Archangels and what each Archangel's role is in people's lives.

Keter - Crown

The crown is overseen by the Archangel Metatron, who, as the angel of life, is the first to receive divine energy. He directs this essence towards the universe brought to life by the Creator, establishing a balance between the different parts of the universe. Metatron can help bring sacred spiritual power into people's lives. He is often revered by those wanting to obtain enlightenment and feels a connection to the divine, even though they can't interact with it directly.

Chokhmah - Wisdom

This sefirah is the dominion of the Archangel Raziel, the angel of mystery and secret. To help people obtain wisdom, Raziel leads them to the revelation of mysteries and truths they were aware of. Not only that, but Raziel also demonstrates to people how to use their newfound wisdom in practical ways. This Archangel is called on (through the Sefirot) by people wanting to reach their full potential or find the purpose the Creator bestowed upon them.

Binah - Understanding

Understanding is the sefirah ruled by the Archangel Tzaphkiel. As the angel of compassion and spiritual energy, Tzaphkiel is responsible for helping people understand the essence of the divine. He instructs people about the Creator, offering insights about his children (the people themselves and all living beings). Tzaphkiel is called on by people wanting to ensure their decisions align with their core identity.

Chesed - Mercy

This sefirah is illuminated by the Archangel Zadkiel, who, as the angel of mercy, ensures that God's mercy is equally distributed across the entire universe. He inspires people to find kindness towards others and show mercy, just as the Creator does with them. Zadkiel also helps people find peace through prayer by showing them that their prayers will be answered – as long as it's in their best interest.

Geburah - Strength

Led by the Archangel Chamuel, this sefirah is where the true essence of relationships stems from. Chamuel shows people that in order to build a strong relationship, they must be truthful to themselves and others. Having better relationships brings peace into people's lives. For this, the angel tests people's motivations in relationships, purifying them in the process, which ultimately allows them to have a better relationship with the divine.

Tiphareth - Beauty

The sefirah of beauty is the result of the Archangels Raphael and Michael working side by side. As the Creator's favorite angel, Michael helps express divine beauty to people and being the angel of healing, Raphael enables people to find and use beauty to heal themselves. By teaching people, the divine (true) meaning of beauty, this angelic duo allows people to reach a higher level of spiritual consciousness.

Netzach - Eternity

Archangel Haniel oversees eternity. This is the angel of joy, who distributes the divine essence of eternity by showing people they can rely on God. He doesn't expect people to change their emotions. Haniel provides insight that leads people to joy and happiness, regardless of their situations.

Hod - Glory

Also led by the dynamic duo of Michael and Raphael, Hod is the sefirah in which The Creator's glory is expressed. Because glory is beautiful, this branch is tied to beauty. The two Archangels ensure that the glory remains beautiful and victorious by eradicating sin from people's lives. They often help people reveal the meaning of glory in their own lives.

Yesod - Foundation

Foundation is the sefirah in which Gabriel, the angel of revelation, works. His dominion is communication and represents the foundation of people's lives, which is why he's entrusted with the foundation of the sacred tree. Gabriel is in charge of the messages people send to express their faith and the answers that allow them to rely on this faith.

Malkuth - Kingdom

This sefirah is ruled by Salphadon, the angel of prayer and music. This is another angel that helps people communicate with the divine. By allowing people to express their thoughts through other forms of communication, Salphadon facilitates the flow of information, nurturing the divine essence in everyone.

The Main Traits of Jewish Magical Practices

Nowadays, the practices of Jewish mysticism are open to personal interpretation. Some followers of the traditional customs rely only on the secret ancient writings found in the Zohar. Others take the mystical part of their practices more seriously, trying to connect the traditional elements with the magical. These practitioners often use Kabbalistic resources for prayers and magical acts alike. For example, they may have a book of traditional prayers and a book of shadows for spirituality-enhancing magic. Another group may refer only to folk magic, incorporating only a few Kabbalistic elements into their practice. This is usually tied to a specific essence (Sephirot) or energy mentioned in the Kabbalah. Even though they find it more worthwhile to follow the old beliefs, these practitioners often find solace and empowerment in the different divine energies.

Although Jewish magical practices have evolved through history, they remain parallel with the traditional teaching of the Torah. One of the most popular practices is visiting the ancestors' resting places, typically former practitioners (called sages) themselves. Because these sacred sites are believed to contain magical powers, they're often used for empowering spells, charms, and rituals. According to Jewish lore, these places hold elements of folk magic. For example, some are known for their exceptional healing powers, while others are said to help find love. Another practice that continues to this day is making magical amulets. Bracelets and other charms containing sacred inscriptions or symbols like hamsa are often used for healing, protection, warding off the evil eye, and enhancing magical powers.

Astrology is also incorporated into modern Jewish magical practices. The zodiac has served as a central motive for symbolism and divinatory practices. Contemporary practitioners often believe that the divine energy will give them insight into their present and future lives. This information can be found in one's mind or harnessed from the supernatural world made by the Creator. To reveal the former, mystics often use dream divination. However, they advise using prophetic dreams alongside other practices to obtain better results. A person's dreams can be influenced by good intentions, often offering an opportunity to receive spiritual messages. Yet they also are affected by malicious ones, which may lead to distorted prophecies.

While today, most practitioners prefer to invoke angels only, according to written historical evidence, both good and bad spirits were also called upon in the past. However, the same historical records show that very few mystics know how to interact with supernatural beings other than angels. This is why it's not advised to summon them, especially if you are a beginner just delving into this world.

In parallel, spellcasting is another magical act associated with modern Jewish magic. It remains unclear whether mystics used actual spells or incantations in ancient times. However, some consider that spoken magic (as spellcasting is often called) has been present since the beginning of time. Many practitioners believe that the act of creation was the spell cast upon the world. Spells can be used for constructive and destructive purposes, but many prefer using them for negative and truthful purposes only. Spellwork in Jewish magic typically revolves around invoking the divine energy and utilizing it to enrich one's practices and obtain the goal of revealing the truth.

Is Jewish Magic for You?

Because each person is naturally limited in their capacity to absorb the divine power of the Creator and the Torah, everyone must examine their own potential. However, having limited abilities doesn't mean you can't explore where they might take you. If you're wondering whether you have the ability to practice Jewish magic and, if yes, in what capacity, answering the following questions for yourself may help you discover whether this path is for you.

- Do I prefer enhancing my magic with divinatory practices, chants, and incantations?
- Do I use herbs or plants for healing or other purposes?
- Do I invoke just angels for guidance, additional energy, and more, or call on spirits too?
- Do I make and use charms and talismans to empower your practice?

- Do I frequent or wish to visit sites known for being magical energetic sources for Jewish mystics?

If you answered most of the questions positively, you would feel the need to be inspired by the mystical energy of the Torah and Kabbalah. If most of your answers are negative, Jewish magic may not be the right choice for you. However, if your answers are roughly evenly split between the two, you may still have the capacity to become a mystic. Feel free to continue pursuing the practices you feel the calling for.

Chapter 8: Sacred Plants and Herbs

Herbs and plants have always been linked to magic and supernatural lore. For centuries, people have depended on them for their healing abilities. From superficial wounds to serious ailments, they have been a source of healing and comfort. They also play a huge role in the practice of folk magic as well. Seeing as many folk magic practitioners were healers, it makes sense that they incorporated these sacred herbs and plants into many of their healing spells. They also used them in other spells that helped improve their communities and provided solutions for many issues they faced at the time. Practitioners also turn to sacred plants and herbs to connect with the other world and supernatural beings.

Cinnamon is one of the oldest herbs in the world.
https://www.pexels.com/photo/cinnamon-sticks-71128/

Every magic tradition uses sacred plants and herbs. Each of them has a long and rich history in these traditions. For instance, most people associate mistletoe with Christmas decorations and kissing. What you may not know is that mistletoe predates Christmas and has had a great influence on magic for centuries, starting with the Druids' interest in this plant. The same goes for many of the herbs you have in your kitchen. You may think they only serve as spices to make your dish tasty or provide a remedy for common ailments. However, these herbs and plants are more powerful than they look, and you can benefit from their powers just like your ancestors did. In this chapter, we will focus on sacred plants and herbs and learn everything they have to offer.

Chamomile

You may already be familiar with chamomile tea, as it is often recommended for people who need to calm their nerves. Chamomile is a herb that is essentially a beautiful flower with white petals, which you can find in many gardens. This herb is often included in various spells and magical rituals. Chamomile has been a part of the magical world since ancient times. Ancient Egyptians were one of the first cultures to use it, but the English made it popular.

Magic Traditions

It's believed that chamomile was used in Norse Paganism as it was very popular among the Vikings. In fact, it is the plant of Asgard and was mentioned in some of their literary works as well. It is also associated with the Celtic goddess of fertility, Cernunnos. In American folk magic and Hoodoo, chamomile is a popular herb that brings good luck. Before gambling, players often wash their hands in chamomile tea to increase their chances of winning.

Spiritual Meaning

Chamomile is a symbol of positivity, and its flower symbolizes poise and humility. The flower has the ability to make your wishes come true. Many magic traditions have similar interpretations of chamomile, viewing it as an herb that brings good luck.

Magical Practices

Chamomile can cleanse spaces and protect against magical attacks. It is also considered a lucky charm. Practitioners use this herb in banishing rituals as well. Similar to other herbs, chamomile can drive away negative energy and evil spirits. It is also a very popular herb in candle magic.

Practitioners also use it to counteract a spell that was cast against them. It has always been an essential ingredient in prosperity and blessing spells and is also used in other spells and rituals.

- Practitioners use chamomile in spells to attract peace, happiness, and love.
- Practitioners wash their hands with chamomile before practicing any spell to increase their chances of success.
- They use chamomile in ritual baths that often take place before performing any spells.
- Chamomile in ritual baths can also help release negative feelings like anger or pain and help one let go of an old lover.
- Burning chamomile can attract money into one's life.

Cinnamon

Cinnamon is one of the oldest herbs in the world. Its place of origin is Sri Lanka, but other cultures have been using it for centuries. For instance, the ancient Egyptians used cinnamon to mummify their dead. The first people to ever use cinnamon were the Chinese in 2800 BC. In ancient times and now still, cinnamon has been known for its healing properties.

Magic Traditions

As one of the oldest herbs around, cinnamon exists in multiple cultures and magic traditions. It's used in African spirituality to protect people and homes from evil magic. In Curanderismo, Mexican folks use it on the Day of the Dead festival to get rid of negative energy.

Spiritual Meaning

Cinnamon has fiery qualities because it's ruled by Mars and the Sun. For thousands of years, this ancient herb has been a symbol of spirituality, fertility, good health, protection, love, and good luck. Practitioners use cinnamon to bless their magical tools and the space before casting a spell. There is a mysterious connection between cinnamon and the human spirit. Burning this fiery herb can increase one's spiritual powers and enhance their psychic ability. In various magical practices, practitioners seem to value cinnamon mainly for its protective abilities.

Magical Practices

When it comes to love spells, there isn't a better herb to use than cinnamon. It's a powerful aphrodisiac and can stir up feelings of lust between lovers. This is why practitioners often include it in sex magic and love spells. They also use it to bring an old love back. Cinnamon also has protective qualities, which is why people incorporate it into practices that serve to protect from negative energies. Some spells can take longer than others before showing real results. Practitioners who want to speed up the process often use cinnamon to make spells work faster. Cinnamon is also a necessary ingredient in healing spells, spells that bring good luck and those that bring success. Practitioners also include cinnamon in various other practices.

- Burning cinnamon can purify the space.
- Cinnamon can be used as a good luck charm.
- Cinnamon can cleanse and purify your divination tools and charge them with clairvoyant energy. Simply put a cinnamon stick in your tools or runes bag or in your tarot card cloth.
- Practitioners include cinnamon in moon rituals and spells that bring joy and wealth into your life and provide protection.
- Drinking cinnamon beverages can increase practitioners' insight and assist them in divination.
- Practitioners include it in rituals that bring prosperity, success, or whatever a person desires.
- Practitioners use cinnamon in rituals that bring victory.

Frankincense

Frankincense is a type of plant that's considered a magical resin. It grows on trees and is associated with African cultures, among others. People all over the world have been using frankincense for centuries. Cultures that believe in reincarnation bathe newborn babies in frankincense oil to cleanse the baby from past lives' demons.

Magic Traditions

In Hoodoo and rootwork, practitioners use frankincense to bless their petitions. Frankincense has a potent vibrational energy, which is why Hoodoo practitioners often mix it with weaker herbs that could use a magical boost. In African tradition, the scent of frankincense is believed to have the ability to ward off evil spirits.

Spiritual Meaning

For centuries, practitioners have been using frankincense in spiritual rituals. This magical resin symbolizes righteousness and holiness. Various practices use frankincense for its protective qualities.

Magical Practice

Practitioners use frankincense to purify spaces, especially sacred ones. It's also known to bring good luck. They also use it in various spiritual rituals as it wards off negative energies. Healers have used frankincense in healing rituals and remedies since ancient times. Practitioners use frankincense in rituals that allow them to communicate with the other world or the spirits of their ancestors. It's believed that the fragrance of frankincense can get the spirits' attention so they can help the practitioners with their rituals. They also use it to invite good spirits.

Mistletoe

Most people are familiar with mistletoe as it's the famous Christmas decoration under which people often kiss. However, mistletoe is more than just an ornament. Various cultures throughout history have revered this plant. Mistletoe has several magical properties, and it's believed to be a good omen that can provide protection against witchcraft.

Magic Traditions

In Druidism, mistletoe played a big part in magical practices. It was also associated with the Celtic magic tradition, as the Druids highly revered it and considered it a sacred plant. The Druids believed that mistletoe was only powerful and effective when it was still growing on trees. However, it would lose all of its magic if it fell to the ground. For this reason, the Druids climbed on trees to harvest the plant. It's believed that the Druids were the first people to use mistletoe for decoration. To them, mistletoe wasn't an ordinary plant but one that had the ability to perform miracles. The Druids believed that the mistletoe was a symbol of life. They would watch how leaves often withered and fell off trees while the mistletoe thrived, maintaining its beautiful green color. The mistletoe remained vibrant in the middle of dying trees, which is why Druids saw it as a symbol of life and rebirth.

In Norse traditions, mistletoe was considered a good luck charm. In the Voodoo magic tradition, it's used to ward off evil spirits.

Spiritual Meaning

Mistletoe is a symbol of immortality, fertility, rebirth, magic, protection, femininity, peace, healing, and unification. The reason behind all these symbolic attributes is the powerful magic behind them. The plant has both female and male energies. It also symbolizes love, which is why it became a tradition for people to kiss under it. Voodoo, Druids, and Norse practices all had various interpretations of what this plant represented.

Magical Practices

Mistletoe is included in protection spells and ones that bring good luck. Practitioners also used it in spells to encourage forgiveness and attract love. It's commonly used in healing spells and protects against cold winters and various diseases. Other magic practices include:

- Protection against evil spirits, evil witches, and ghosts.
- Practitioners included it in remedies that could cure poison.

Mugwort

Mugwort is an old herb, but it's often used in modern magic practices.

Magic Traditions

Native Americans use mugwort to protect themselves against ghosts. It's also used in Shaman purification rituals.

Spiritual Meaning

Mugwort is associated with the goddess of the moon, Artemis, and is connected to lunar magic. Blending this herb with other herbs can provide a deeply spiritual experience.

Magical Practices

Practitioners use mugwort for various magic practices like smudging, spellwork, and as incense. Mugwort is also used in healing spells. In the past, people believed certain diseases were caused by the Fae (fairies) and that mugwort was the perfect herb to combat this type of disease. It's also used in divination practices to enhance the gift of prophecy. Mugwort is used in ritual baths to help people suffering from overactive dreams.

- Practitioners use mugwort as protection against psychic attacks
- They use it in divination like runes and reading cards
- Practitioners use mugwort to increase their psychic abilities
- Practitioners use mugwort in protective spells against evil spirits

- They use it in tea leaf reading
- They use it to cleanse divination tools
- They include it in incense rituals
- It's used to invite good spirits

Rosemary

Ancient practitioners valued rosemary highly, as they knew what this herb had to offer. At the time, rosemary was one of the most effective herbs for brain and memory issues. It isn't an exaggeration to say that every practitioner must always carry rosemary with them, as it can replace many herbs in spellwork. There is a misconception that since rosemary is used in witchcraft, it may not be safe to use in other types of magic. However, there's nothing harmful or evil about rosemary, and it's commonly used in various folk practices all over the world.

Magic Traditions

Several magic traditions around the world use rosemary as protection against evil witches and spirits. In Hoodoo magic, practitioners use rosemary for its protective properties. They believe it protects them against evil spirits and brings good fortune. It's also believed that this herb guarantees that a marriage will be long and happy and that both partners will remain faithful to each other. Rosemary is also popular among Druidry practices, where people use it to communicate with their ancestors and sharpen their minds. They also used it to attract fairies.

Spiritual Meaning

Rosemary is a symbol of spirituality and longevity. Back in the day, if rosemary was grown in someone's kitchen or garden, this meant that the lady of the house was the one in charge. According to mythology, this is the only way rosemary would flourish and grow. This herb has always been a symbol of memory and remembrance. For that reason, people often place it in graves to signify that they'll never forget their departed. Rosemary was also considered a symbol of love in ancient times. People believed that by placing the herb under their pillow, they would see the person they were meant to be with in a dream. Rosemary also symbolizes everlasting love, which is why many brides wear it on their wedding day. It's also associated with faith, and many people use it when struggling with their beliefs. It can also prevent people from committing sins as it protects their souls and helps them resist temptation.

Different traditions have various interpretations of this herb. For instance, Hoodoo practitioners use it for its protective properties, while Druidry practitioners use it for divination and visionary work.

Magical Practices

Practitioners burn rosemary in front of their homes to protect them against thieves and anyone who wishes them harm. They also use it against bad omens and energies. It can also be an effective tool to cleanse the interior of homes. Rosemary is one of the most essential ingredients in spells to ward off evil spirits. Since it's a symbol of love, practitioners use it in love potions. Burning rosemary at home can drive away bad luck and attract good fortune. This herb is also a part of spells, rituals, and divination practices that provide healing and increase psychic abilities and spirituality. It's also used in other magical practices.

- Practitioners use rosemary in healing spells
- Rosemary is used in love potions to help people find true love
- Practitioners use it as a protection against bad events
- Rosemary is an essential ingredient in spells that invoke passion
- It's used in spells that can bring back an old love

Sage

Sage is one of the most popular herbs around. For thousands of years, people have used it to make herbal tea, as an ingredient in different recipes, and in various magical practices. Sage is known to be a healing plant, which is where its name comes from. The word sage is derived from "salvare," a Latin word that means "to heal."

Magic Traditions

Sage originates in European traditions. People would dry and smudge it and use it in cleansing ceremonies. European practitioners also used it to drive away evil spirits and protect their communities. They also used it as a good luck charm, and some people believed it could grant them immortality. Native American and Europeans use sage for its healing properties and as protection against evil. African traditions use African sage for cleansing, purification, and protection against evil spirits and negative energies. They also use it in divination and to communicate with their ancestors. Other cultures that use sage include the Inuit, Metis, and First Nations.

Spiritual Meaning

People all over the world have been using sage for its healing and spiritual properties for thousands of years. Ancient cultures used sage to protect them from evil spirits. They also considered sage to be a symbol of wisdom as people believed it had the power to grant them wisdom. The popularity of sage hasn't withered away. To this day, people believe in sage's protective abilities and use them to purify their homes of negative energies. In African traditions, people use African sage for the same spiritual practices and also as protection against ill-intended individuals.

Magical Practices

The most common practice for sage is smudging. Smudging is a Native American practice that works on cleansing a place, person, or group of people from negative energy. It's often done before spiritual work. You'll need a bundle of sage for this ritual. Light the tips with a match, let it burn for a few seconds, and then blow it out. Direct the smoke toward the person or space you want to cleanse. Practitioners also use sage for various other practices.

- Burning sage during funerals can help grieving families and create a bond between the mourners and the spirit of the deceased
- Scattering fresh or dried sage outdoors can bless the area
- Sage is the main ingredient in wisdom-granting spells
- Putting sage under a pillow can protect against nightmares
- Placing sage in your wallet can increase prosperity
- Practitioners use sage in spells that help a person get over someone or end an unhealthy infatuation
- Placing dry sage around a blue candle can calm the spirit

One of the most interesting things about sacred plants and herbs in folk magic is that they all protect against evil spirits. At the time, evil spirits were a real concern among communities. These herbs and plants served as protective tools and to put people's minds at ease. Nowadays, people have other fears and concerns besides evil spirits, like negative energies and people that want them harm. Using sacred herbs and plants can provide a solution to many of these issues.

We can't forget about their healing properties as well. Many of the folk magic practitioners were healers and cunning folks who used herbs and plants to diagnose diseases and heal their communities. In a later chapter, you'll learn various spells that you can perform using these sacred plants and herbs.

Chapter 9: Signs, Symbols, and Charms

This chapter enlists the most common charms used in the different practices mentioned in the previous chapters. First, you'll be presented with a list of symbols, and it will be up to you to decide which one you feel drawn to. Just look at them, and trust your gut to tell you which would be useful. In case you haven't yet determined which tradition aligns with your values, examining the symbols each practice is associated with will help you make a confident decision.

Here is the list of symbols to go over:

1. The Celtic knot

The Celtic knot.

Eugenio Hansen, OFS, CC BY-SA 4.0 <https://creativecommons.org/licenses/by-sa/4.0>, via Wikimedia Commons: https://commons.wikimedia.org/wiki/File:Triquetra-circle-interlaced-black.svg

2. The Celtic cross

The Celtic cross.
GabrielGGD, CC0, via Wikimedia Commons:
https://commons.wikimedia.org/wiki/File:Celtic_Crosses.svg

3. The Triquetra

The Triquetra.
https://commons.wikimedia.org/wiki/File:Triquetra-Vesica.svg

4. The five-fold symbol

The five-fold symbol.
https://commons.wikimedia.org/wiki/File:20-crossings-ornamental-knot.svg

5. The spiral

The spiral.
https://commons.wikimedia.org/wiki/File:Triple-Spiral-Symbol-heavystroked.svg

6. Ankh

Ankh.
Alexi Helligar, CC BY-SA 3.0 <https://creativecommons.org/licenses/by-sa/3.0>, via Wikimedia Commons: https://commons.wikimedia.org/wiki/File:Ankh_(SVG)_01.svg

7. Winged Sun

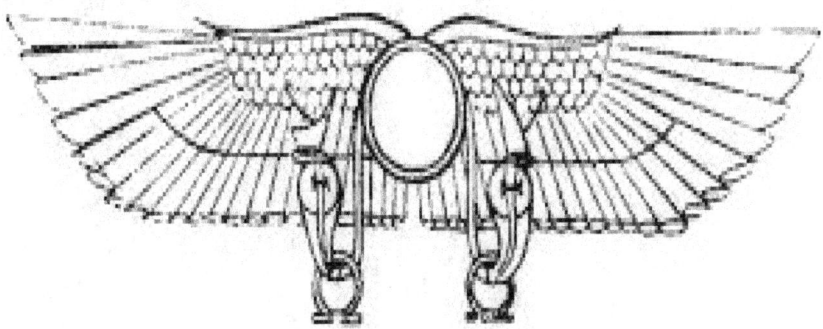

Winged Sun.
https://commons.wikimedia.org/wiki/File:Winged_sun_sharpe.png

8. Adinkra

Adinkra.
kasahorow from Openclipart, CC0, via Wikimedia Commons:
https://commons.wikimedia.org/wiki/File:Gye_Nyame_(Adinkra_Symbol).svg

9. The serpent

The serpent.
https://commons.wikimedia.org/wiki/File:Sea_Serpent_after_Owen_1741.png

10. The helm of Awe

The helm of Awe.
https://commons.wikimedia.org/wiki/File:Aegishjalmr.svg

11. The Hamsa

The Hamsa.
first version Fluff This W3C-unspecified vector image was created with Adobe Illustrator.new version from 2011 Perhelion This W3C-unspecified vector image was created with Inkscape ., CC BY 3.0 <https://creativecommons.org/licenses/by/3.0>, via Wikimedia Commons https://commons.wikimedia.org/wiki/File:WPVA-khamsa.svg

12. The Evil Eye

The Evil Eye.
https://commons.wikimedia.org/wiki/File:Evil_eye.svg

13. The Tree of Life

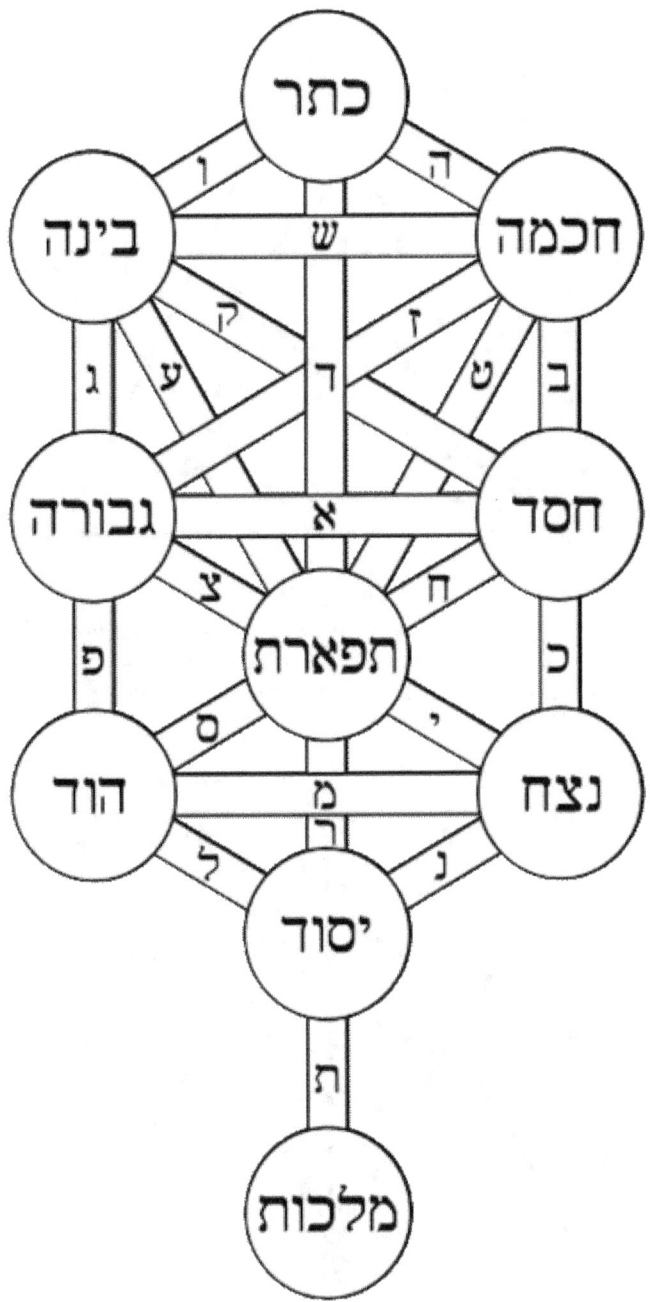

The Tree of Life.
https://commons.wikimedia.org/wiki/File:Tree_of_life_bahir_Hebrew.svg

14. Merkabah

Merkabah.
Joshua Free (creator of the concept), Ony Yahontov (creator of the file)., CC BY-SA 3.0 <https://creativecommons.org/licenses/by-sa/3.0>, via Wikimedia Commons: https://commons.wikimedia.org/wiki/File:Zuist_merkabah.svg

15. The Veves

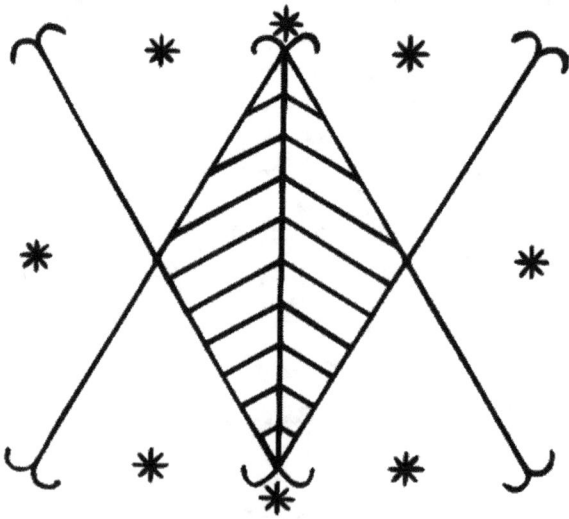

The Veves.
https://commons.wikimedia.org/wiki/File:VeveAyizan.svg

16. Yggdrasil

Yggdrasil.
FrostZERO, CC BY-SA 3.0 <http://creativecommons.org/licenses/by-sa/3.0/>, via Wikimedia Commons: https://commons.wikimedia.org/wiki/File:DesenhodabandaYggDrasil.jpg

17. The Triskele

The Triskele.
https://commons.wikimedia.org/wiki/File:Triskele-Symbol1.svg

18. Mjolnir

Mjolnir.
https://commons.wikimedia.org/wiki/File:Mjollnir.png

19. Vegvisir

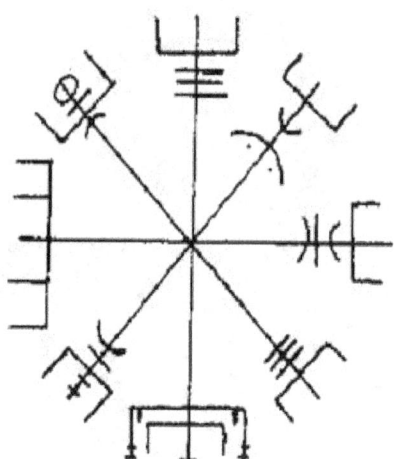

Vegvisir.
Jara Lisa, CC BY-SA 4.0 <https://creativecommons.org/licenses/by-sa/4.0>, via Wikimedia Commons https://commons.wikimedia.org/wiki/File:Vegvisir_de_Steven_Flowers.png

20. Valknut

Valknut.
https://commons.wikimedia.org/wiki/File:9crossings-knot-symmetric-triangles-quasi-valknut.svg

The Meaning of the Symbols

Now that you've had a chance to look at the symbols without a preconceived notion, you can delve into their purposes and applications. Here is a little background about them and their uses in their respective traditions.

1. The Celtic Knot

The Celtic knot is probably one of the most recognizable Pagan symbols. Typically presented as a series of knots forming a unique pattern, the symbol is often used in Celtic magic and Druidic practices. The Celtic knot can be found in religious manuscripts and architecture, representing the limitless power of the divine. In Celtic magic practices, it symbolizes the life cycle, birth, death, and rebirth, present in nature and human lives alike. You can incorporate it into different traditions designed to call on nature's infinite power, rejuvenation spells and rituals, fertility rites, and much more.

2. The Celtic Cross

After the Celtic Knot, the Celtic cross is the second most famous symbol utilized in traditional Pagan magic practices. It can also be found in architecture and monuments carved into stone. They can also be seen as independent stone monoliths made from wood or metal and shaped like a cross. In Celtic magic, the symbol has several interpretations. According to one, the four arms of the cross represent the four natural elements, water, fire, earth, and air. Another source showcases the symbol as the illustration of the four cardinal directions, east, west, north, and south. Apart from representing these, you can use the Celtic cross in your practices to represent the four seasons, the four stages of the day, or anything with four aspects.

3. The Triquetra

The triquetra is another Celtic pagan symbol used in Celtic magical traditions. It can be portrayed in several ways, usually in some form of three interlaced shapes, like Vesica Pisces or arcs. The symbol is often found in Celtic art, sometimes with a circle around it. The meaning of the three arcs varies depending on which interpretation you want to follow. For example, you can use it to represent and honor the Triple Goddess. It can also be employed to call on the power of the world's three realms of the world: sky, sea, and land.

4. The Five-Fold Symbol

The five-fold symbol also has Celtic pagan origins, but it's also often found in Scottish magic. According to ancient Scottish transitions, the symbol represents the different aspects contributing to the balance of human lives. In contemporary practices, it's often used to illustrate the four elements, fire, water, air, and earth, tied together by a fifth element, the universe itself. You can also use it to represent the four elements and the spirit or the five pillars of the universe, earth, air, sun, fire, and water.

5. The Spiral

Similarly to the previous one, the single spiral is also found in Scottish magic and was also a fundamental part of the ancient Celtic pagan culture. Physically illustrating a shape folded onto itself, the spiral represents infinite energy. Its waves are seen radiating outside, giving life to several different essences. According to one interpretation, the symbol showcases a person's life and the wisdom they've gathered from birth through life to death. You can also use it to gain awareness of your present and surroundings, to persevere against challenges, or to gather spiritual knowledge.

6. Ankh

Ankh is a crucial element in several African spiritual practices. It is believed to represent immortality and the divine mother, Isis. Nowadays, the symbol is used as the representation of life or the key to obtaining immortal life. It's incorporated into spiritual practices designed to elevate your level of consciousness, helping you reach a higher plane and become enlightened with infinite wisdom.

7. Winged Sun Disk

The winged sun disk symbol is also used in African spirituality as the representation of the sun god, or the sun itself, depending on the interpretation. If you're using it to honor the sun god, you're representing the creator of the universe. However, if you want to showcase the celestial body, you're celebrating life itself. Because without the sun, there wouldn't be life on earth. It can also be incorporated into practices for seeking spiritual elevation.

8. Adinkra

Adinkra is a symbol not unlike a simple drawing of a fern. It's used in African cultures. It's typically printed or painted on clothes, charms, and jewelry, often seen as a demonstration of spiritual power. Wearing this symbol will suggest to people that you're in control of your fate and will not let anyone else influence your life with their negative vibes. The symbol also means you have plans, love to work with people, and you'll do everything to obtain your goals.

9. The Serpent

The serpent is one of the most ancient symbols, and as such, it is used in different traditions. However, its most notable use is in Brujeria and Curanderismo, where it is integrated into transformative and healing spells and rituals. It's typically placed at the altar, in the middle of a protective circle, or onto any other sacred surface you use to perform your magical act. As a powerful being, the serpent will help you transform your life, go through a rebirth physically, mentally, and spiritually, and bring fertility into any area of your life.

10. The Helm of Awe

Also known as Aegishjalmur, the Helm of Awe is an ancient Norse symbol primarily used by Norse warriors who painted them on their forehead before going to a battle. Upon closer inspection, the symbol is seen as the combination of Isa and Algiz, two runes from the Elder

Futhark. Isa symbolizes self-preservation, focus, and challenge. Whereas Algiz inspires victory and protection. In contemporary practices, this combined effect is used for empowerment when facing an illness, injury, or stressful situation. It can also help you ward off evil intentions, just as it worked to induce fear in the enemies of the Viking tribes. The symbol is shaped like a circle, which represents protection. The eight branches will ensure you can ward off evil intent no matter which direction it comes from. It'll help you overcome any challenge and become more aware of your own power.

11. The Hamsa

The word "hamsa" means "five" in Arabic, indicating the five fingers of a hand. The Hamsa is the symbol of protection in Jewish magic, and according to Kabbalah, it was used to invoke divine power, represented by the hand of God. Nowadays, it's still used for similar purposes, including in prayers and Kabbalistic rituals for different purposes. It is believed to protect against the Evil Eye (if that symbol is used for malicious intent) or evil in general. Use it within the scope of spells and rituals when you need an added layer of protection or when your energy is out of balance and you want to invite peace back into your life.

12. The Evil Eye

As mentioned above, envious people can use the Evil Eye to induce harm. However, it can also be helpful for warding off this type of energy. If you have anyone in your life that looks at your success and wonders what you have done to deserve this, their symbol will help you ward off their jealousy. It's recommended to wear it as a talisman whenever you interact with this person, and they'll soon cease their behavior. For added power, make sure you imbue the charm with the intention of keeping that person at bay. You can also combine it with other protective elements incorporated in Jewish folk magic traditions, such as wearing the charm on a red string bracelet.

13. The Tree of Life

While the tree of life is present in several traditions, in Jewish mysticism, it has a unique and powerful meaning. In Kabbalah, the Tree of Life is represented as a tree with ten branches, also referred to as the ten Sefirot. The ten Sefirot illustrate the different divine essence, the only form of God people can perceive and interact with. The symbol is used to invoke either one of these divine emanations through its rulers, the Archangels. Depending on which energy you need in your practice, you'll call on the Archangel that allows its distribution through the universe from their respective dominion.

14. Merkabah

A veve is a representation of an energetic force in African spiritual practices. These forces are spirits associated with elements of nature, its different powers, values, and emotions. The veves were initially made from flour or other powdery substance, which allowed people to invite the spirits' energy to one dedicated area. You can also draw or print veves on paper or any other surface and use them to attract a particular entity. Focusing on it will help you get them to reveal themselves in front of you.

15. The Veves

A veve is a representation of an energetic force in African spiritual practices. These are spirits associated with elements of nature, its different forces, values, and emotions. The veves are drawings, initially made from flour or other powdery substance, which allowed people to invite the spirits' energy to one dedicated area. You can also draw or print veves on paper or any other surface and use them to attract a particular entity. Focusing on it will help you get them to reveal themselves in front of you.

16. Yggdrasil

Yggdrasil, also called the Norse Tree of Life, is somewhat different from its Jewish counterpart. Not only does it have only nine branches (representing the nine realms of Norse mythology), but it has various tales and uses tied to it. According to one of these tales, Yggdrasil grew from the Well of Urd, the universal source of life. It's also believed that the Norse deities were eating their fruit to remain immortal. You can use Yggdrasil in rituals and spells where you want to make a connection to nature and the universe or reveal parts of your future. When used in meditation, it can also help you balance out your energies.

17. The Triskele

The Triskele, or the Horns of Odin, as it is called in Norse traditions, is a symbol with Celtic pagan origins. It's usually linked to Odin and his infinite power and wisdom. Hold it above your drink or meal and focus on infusing those with his power. When you consume some of it, you'll empower your own magic. It can also help you improve your communication skills and establish new connections in any area of your life.

18. Mjolnir

While most people are familiar with Mjolnir being the hammer of Thor, very few are aware of the magical significance of this tool. In ancient times, the Norse attributed lighting to Mjolnir being used against giants, their feared enemies. Therefore, Thor's hammer has become a symbol of protection, as it's used in modern Norse magical practices too. When incorporated into protection rituals and spells you perform before you begin to work, it can safeguard you from malicious intent during magical work. Wear it as a talisman, a charm, or a necklace, and it will also protect you in your day-to-day life.

19. Vegvisir

Vegvisir is a Norse symbol with eight branches held up by a central pillar. There are several interpretations of what the branches mean. According to one, they represent the expanded directions, south, southwest, southeast, north, northwest, northeast, west, and east. Another lore says the branches represent eight out of the nine worlds of Norse mythology, with the center being the ninth world. In modern times, practitioners use this symbol for guidance when they aren't sure if they're headed in the right direction or have lost their way completely. You can also wear it as a talisman, and it'll protect you just as it did the Viking ships during vicious storms. It can also guide you through challenging situations or when you feel you've lost part of yourself due to emotional trauma. It will boost your confidence in your ability to persevere against the odds, allowing you to achieve this goal. Another way to incorporate the symbol into your practice is to enhance it with magic and give it to someone as a good luck charm to attract love and prosperity.

20. Valknut

Valknut, or Odin's knot, as it's called in Norse mythology, is the ultimate symbol of death. It was used to honor the fallen warriors and help them cross onto Valhalla, Hel, and other afterlife realms. According to another interpretation, Valknut can provide protection for the souls who passed on. Wearing it as a talisman, you can also use it to draw Odin's power to help you with spiritual communication. It will shield you and the friendly spirit you are trying to contact through the realms from malicious spirits.

Infusing the Symbols with Magic

Once you've found the symbol or symbols you wish to use in your craft, you must prepare them and yourself for their use. The first step in this process is cleansing your mind and body. This will ensure that your power remains pure, and you won't have any negative vibes affecting the symbols' magic. You can do this by taking a cleaning bath, performing breathing exercises, smudging your body, or through any other purification ritual of your choice. Smudging can also be used to eradicate any negative influence from the room or space you'll use or set up your magical tools. Smudging is a simple process that involves lighting a small bunch of dried herbs on fire and letting their smoke permeate and cleanse every corner of your space. When doing this, move around to ensure no negative energy remains, and pass over the symbols several times.

Once you've ascertained that the symbols are ready to be infused with positive energy, you can focus on this task. Be as clear and concise as possible when forming an intention. This will make the process smoother. For example, if you want a character to serve as protection, you'll need to express this. You'll need to say that you need the symbol to carry protective magic. If you require healing, a good luck charm, attracting love, or financial prosperity, then you ask for those. Depending on your purpose and experience, you may need more time to infuse the symbols with the desired form of magic. There are several ways to go about when doing this, and the choice will often depend on your intention and personal preferences. Here are some techniques to imbue symbols with magic:

- **Meditation:** This approach takes only a few minutes a day and allows you to submerge into your thoughts while keeping the symbol or charm in your hands. Take a deep breath and focus on sending your energy toward the sign. It also helps awaken the character's own magic. You can either close your eyes and visualize the symbols in front of you or keep them open and look at the symbol until it's ready to use.

- **Journeying:** Similarly to meditation, journeying also requires a deep focus, which will help focus your thoughts on the symbol and your intention. During your journey, you may also ask a spiritual guide to help you empower the sign you are holding in your hands.

- **Prayers and offerings:** If you're working with a higher spiritual being, or your symbol is associated with them, you can ask them to give you the ability to infuse the magical tool with your intent, magic, and perhaps their magic too. Prayers and offerings are great ways to express gratitude for whatever help you get from the symbols.
- **Dreams:** Keeping symbols near your body while sleeping is an ancient tradition that involves the activation of magical tools. You can draw or print symbols on paper and place them under your pillow. Or, you can put the tool or charm on your nightstand, look at them before going to sleep, repeat your intention in your head, and go to bed.
- **Using celestial bodies:** Many cultures use the power of the sun and the moon to enrich and activate magical tools. This is usually combined with other intention-boosting and charm-activating techniques. For example, you can place the symbols under the moonlight at the full moon and meditate on your intention by sitting nearby and gazing at the moon.
- **Using the elements:** The natural and celestial elements can also be used to infuse magical tools like symbols with positive intentions and magic. For this, you'll need an altar or any other sacred space where you can place the sign and the representations of the elements around it. Ask the elements to help consecrate the symbols and allow you to channel your intention toward them.
- **Wearing them:** Some symbols will benefit from staying close to your body. This will ensure your intention is engraved into them. It also works for infusing personal magic. There are symbols you can keep wearing on or near your body even after they've been infused with magic, especially if the spell or ritual they are used in requires this. You can also draw a symbol on a piece of paper and put it in your pocket or bag for the required duration.

How long it takes to prepare your symbols depends on several factors. It may take more time to ensure they are ready to use before you delve into any magical practice. Check this by feeling their energy. If it's aligned with yours and you can feel their magic, you're good to go. If not, you'll need to put more effort into infusing the symbols. You'll need to truly want it to lead you to your goals, so keep your focus on the task and trust your intuition. It will show you the way, as no other guide will ever be able to.

Chapter 10: Your Folk Magic Spellbook

Rituals and spellwork can seem complicated at the beginning, and feeling lost during this time is completely normal for someone just starting on this journey. Spellwork is broadly defined as the technique of using certain words and gestures in combination with herbs, candles, or other charms and symbols. Spellwork has always been an important part of folk magic cultures and religions. It is the foundation of folk magic, helping draw energy from a different plane of existence. This energy is then imbued into this world by using sacred words, gestures, and other practices.

Spellwork has always been an important part of folk magic cultures and religions.

https://www.pexels.com/photo/a-spell-book-and-gem-stone-on-the-window-seal-6806397/

Spellwork is a lot like physical exercise. As consistency and practice help strengthen your muscles, the same goes for spellwork. When you repeat and practice a spell consistently, you'll ultimately be able to manifest your desires. As you continue practicing various spells, you'll find yourself working alongside your intuition and, soon enough, mastering the art of spellwork. Often, you may not get the results you desire from rituals and spellwork, but don't let this discourage you. Just because a spell works for one person does not mean it will work for another.

The accuracy and flow of your spellwork will improve with time and practice, but you have to start somewhere. This chapter will act as a beginner's guide to spellwork and rituals as practiced in various folk magic cultures.

Wiccan Celtic Magic

To Honor a Deceased Loved One

Intent: To honor a deceased loved one and deal with your grief. This ritual will help you cope with the loss you've experienced.

Things You'll Need

- A picture of your deceased loved one. Make sure it is a spare photo or a copy you won't miss
- Some memorabilia of your loved one, such as a necklace, ring, or some other piece associated with them
- Your preferred drink, coffee, tea, or anything else
- A thin, medium-sized, white candle
- A lighter or matches
- A marker or pen

Method

1. Choose a day for the ritual. It should be a day you associate with your loved one, like their death anniversary or their birthday.
2. Sit in a comfortable place along with the supplies you've gathered for this ritual.
3. Light the candle, pour your favorite beverage, and relax in the moment. Erase all thoughts from your mind. Only think of the person you've lost and let yourself feel the grief.
4. Take a sip from your drink, and start writing a personal letter to your deceased loved one on the back of their picture. Write down

everything you wanted to say to them, and bid them farewell.
5. At the end of the letter, write: "The meaning of this spell will be gone but never forgotten."
6. After you're done with the letter, read it aloud to get it across to the spirit of your loved one.
7. Finish your drink while letting the candle burn out, then fold the picture as many times as you can.
8. Keep this picture safe, and when you visit the grave of your loved one, bury it near their gravestone along with the memorabilia.

Purification Spell

Intent: to eliminate a negative feeling, entity, situation, or person from your life.

What You'll Need
- Sea salt
- A lighter or matches
- Cumin
- A black colored ribbon
- A pen and paper
- A glass jar
- A small dish
- An offering or item associated with the person or situation you're trying to remove

Method
1. Take a small jar and place some cumin inside it until it's half full.
2. Then, take a spoonful of sea salt and place it on top of the cumin.
3. Take a piece of paper and write down the name, feeling, or situation that is troubling you. Put this paper in a non-flammable dish and light it.
4. Once the paper has burned completely, take the ashes from the dish and place them on top of the sea salt inside the glass jar.
5. Fasten the lid of the jar as tightly as you can, and every night before bed, shake this jar as many times as you want. While you do this, picture the situation or person slowly moving away from your life. Repeat this until the next full moon.

6. Once the full moon arrives, tie the black ribbon around the glass jar and go to a river, beach, or lake.
7. Either throw or place the glass jar into the water along with the offering you've selected and watch it drift away. Walk away from this place without looking back.

Recovery Spell

Intent: To help yourself recover from whatever troubles you've faced and gain your sense of self-worth back. This spell is ideal for healing from a traumatic event.

What You'll Need
- Thyme
- Mint
- Sea salt or pink Himalayan salt
- Rose quartz
- A lily
- A rose
- Some bay leaves
- Olive oil
- Cinnamon
- A small sealable jug or bottle
- A cooking pot
- Some water

Method
1. Fill the cooking pot with water and put it on the stove to heat.
2. Once the water has boiled, add the flower petals from the rose and lily flowers. Next, add a pinch of Himalayan salt and some oil into the boiling water. Keep mixing as you add the ingredients.
3. Finally, add the thyme, mint, and cinnamon into the pot and stir slowly. While you're stirring, say the words:
4. "I forgive myself and love myself despite everything that's happened to me. I accept the suffering and let it move forward with me. My past doesn't define me, and neither does my pain or misfortune. I accept myself as I am and let my inner light shine through."

5. Repeat this spell three times while slowly stirring the potion, and pour it into the jar when it's done.
6. Later that day, take this potion and add it to your shower or bath routine while holding the rose quartz crystal. This will ensure that all your negative energy is sucked out and your energy is replenished.
7. Keep this bottle with you, and use it whenever you need to recover or heal from something.

African Spirituality

Gris Gris

Intent: Gris Gris bags are used to bring you prosperity and fortune. These mojo bags are considered the most powerful piece of charm in Voodoo magic. They assist in all matters of life with the right intent by empowering their owners. Many consider it a prayer in a bag.

What You'll Need
- A piece of fabric
- A string or elastic band
- Some sacred herbs of your choice (basil, lavender, dandelion, ivy, marigold, or any other herbs mentioned in the previous chapters)
- A few crystals (Quartz, tourmaline, emerald, selenite, malachite, or any other crystals of your choice)
- Shells or unique stones
- Talismans or charms of your choice
- A small candle

Method
1. Gather all the materials and sit in a comfortable space to make your Gris Gris bag.
2. Light the candle first, and lay out the piece of fabric on the floor or on a table.
3. Place each item you've selected on top of the fabric, one at a time.
4. When placing each item onto the fabric, set your intention onto that charm and then place it inside. For instance, you can set the intent for attracting love, prosperity, success, or anything that you

desire.

5. Bring all four corners of the fabric together at the top so that the fabric forms a small bag, and tie it up using a long string.

Crossroads Magic

Intent: Crossroads magic is one of the most powerful sources of sacred practice in Hoodoo and Voodoo magic cultures. Crossroads are where two roads intersect. According to folklore, the crossroads of conjure is where the real world and the spirit world connect. Therefore, crossroads of any kind hold a special value in ancient magic practices. One such spell ensures that all blockages from your path are eliminated.

What You'll Need
- Twenty-one coins or pennies
- Three red candles
- Lighter or matches

Method

1. Find a crossroad that you think best portrays the current situation of your life that's troubling you.
2. Stand in the middle of the crossroad and set the intent of the ritual. Visualize the difficulties you're facing, and count all the obstacles in your path.
3. Place the coins at the crossroad along with the three red candles.
4. Light the candles and wait for them to burn out while you chant some spells.
5. As the candles burn out, visualize all the obstacles and troubles being erased from your path or your "crossroads."

Brujeria and Curanderismo

Los Siete Nudos (The Seven Knots)

Intent: Perform this unique ritual to eliminate seven problems in your life. It will help either solve or eliminate these issues.

What You'll Need
- A red ribbon (2 ft)
- A candle
- A small jar

Method
1. Sit in a comfortable position where you won't be disturbed for the entirety of the ritual.
2. Take the ribbon in your hands, and visualize seven problems that need to be solved in your life.
3. Think of each problem individually, and while doing so, tie a knot in the ribbon.
4. The first knot should be right in the middle of the complete length of the ribbon.
5. The second and third knots should be about four inches to the left and right of the first knot, respectively.
6. The fourth and fifth knots should be four inches away from the second and third knots.
7. The sixth knot should be on the left side of the ribbon, towards the end. Lastly, the seventh knot should connect one end of the ribbon to the other end, binding the problems that trouble you.
8. Place this ribbon into the jar and seal it. Bury the jar far away from where you live to make sure it doesn't get dug up. Also, ensure that you do this ritual alone, or else the spell won't be as effective.

Agua Bendita (Holy Water)

Intent: As an all-purpose, healing, recovery, and protection product, holy water is the best way to cleanse your soul. The quality of holy water depends on how the ritual is carried out.

What You'll Need
- A stick of palo santo (holy wood)
- A silver bullion
- A copper container

Method
1. Place the copper container where there's rainwater in order to collect enough to prepare the holy water. Make sure you collect clear, pure rainwater and not drain water.
2. Place the silver bullion and palo santo stick in the water, and allow them to permeate the water.
3. Once you feel the water has been infused properly, expose it to direct sunlight, where it will gather the energy of light.

4. Finally, pour the holy water into a glass bottle and use it to anoint or asperge the patient during treatment.

Norse Spellwork

Healing Magic

Intent: To heal any sufferings, diseases, or ailments incurred. This spell will help cure any illness or injury.

What You'll Need

- The sacred cauldron
- Mountain ash berries
- Vervain
- Feverfew
- Candles and matches
- A parchment and pencil

Method

1. This ritual is best performed during the waning moon phase. Start by placing the offerings on a platter, and light the candle. These should include the above-mentioned herbs or any alternative herbs.
2. On the piece of parchment, draw a rough sketch of the sick or injured person. This drawing does not need to be perfect; even the sketch of a stick figure will do. Don't forget to write their name at the bottom of the parchment.
3. Now, tap the cauldron with a wand, and chant the following spell:
4. "Oh great cauldron of rebirth and renewal, hear my call and heal (name) of all sickness. Rebuild their body, spirit, and mind."
5. Next, tap the piece of parchment with your wand three times and set it aflame using the candle. Drop this parchment into the cauldron and let it burn. While it's burning, chant this:
6. "All illness turns to ashes; all that was wrong is now right; my words have reached Asgard; your healing will come tonight."
7. Once the parchment turns to ashes, add the herb offerings into the cauldron and let it cool.
8. Finally, take the ashes and herbs and bury them in the ground to eliminate the illness.

Love Spell

Intent: To bring you the love you desire, whether romantic or otherwise. This love spell is incredibly potent and effective.

What You'll Need

- The sacred cauldron
- A pink candle
- A candle holder
- A red rose
- A vase
- Rose blossom oil
- A small bell

Method

1. The altar for this spell should be set up two days in advance before the full moon. Place the pink candle inside the candle holder and put it in the cauldron. The red rose will go into the vase, which will be kept beside the cauldron.
2. On the night of the full moon, start the ritual by grabbing the handle with both hands and pouring feelings of love into it. Do not light the candle before the full moon appears.
3. Use a knife or dagger to carve a rune of true love on the candle and place the candle inside the cauldron. Finally, light the candle, and ring the bell three times. Chant:
4. "As the flame of this candle grows brighter, Freyre, lord of love, please bring me love's ever-burning fire. Then, as the flame flickers low, Freyre, do give to me a true love, heart to heart."
5. Ring the bell three more times, and stay at the altar until the candle has completely burned out.

Spellwork is indeed a delicate part of magic and should be done with the utmost care and focus. While it does take a while to practice, once you're familiar with the processes, you'll start to see real outcomes from your practice. However, make sure you don't rush the process of learning spellwork, rituals, and herb magic. This is something that requires time, patience, and, most importantly, skill.

Conclusion

Folk magic has been a part of human culture since early civilizations, but it was deemed an acceptable practice only recently. While many people often associate magic with Wiccan or Pagan cultures, its scope is, in reality, much greater. It includes Norse paganism, African spirituality, Jewish magic, and countless other magic-practicing cultures. Hopefully, reading this book will have provided you with a clearer picture of what folk magic is and how it lives on. For many people, learning about these practices is often life-changing. This is because it finally allows them to know which culture they most connect with and get to start their journey along this path.

Once you select which folk magic practice to follow, you'll go through tremendous personal changes as your entire belief system matures and evolves. Moreover, you'll find a community full of supportive and encouraging people who'll help you along your journey. At times, the multitude of ideas and concepts may overwhelm you, so make sure you don't lose your way. To master any subject, you must understand the fundamental concepts, and magic practices are no exception. Once you've learned the basics of a specific folk magic culture, nothing can stop you from becoming an expert.

We suggest you go through the last three chapters in detail to avoid any mistakes while practicing, especially if it's your first attempt. The sacred plants and herbs in any culture are sacred for a reason, as they provide numerous benefits and play a special role in magic rituals. Learning about these herbs will be the first step to mastering the art of spells and rituals.

Once you've learned the signs, symbols, and charms associated with each culture, you'll be in a much better position to understand more complex spells and rituals. Also, make sure to follow the spells provided in the last chapter as precisely as you can. Altering even the smallest step can end up making the spell impotent or completely useless.

Once you've grasped a broad understanding of these folk magic cultures, you can move on to learning about the one or ones you're most interested in. By now, you know their history and basics, but there's still a lot to learn. So, as you start on this journey of great spiritual learning, don't hold yourself back from getting all the information required. Most of all, start practicing the traditions that speak to you, which will bring you one step closer to discovering your true self.

Lastly, but importantly, remember that those who practice magic (of any kind) often form close-knit communities. If you ever feel you cannot grasp a particular concept, or perform a specific ritual or spell, don't hesitate to reach out to those who you think may offer assistance. In the meantime, keep this book by your side whenever you need to revisit the fundamentals of folk magic. Good luck!

Part 2: Gypsy Magic

The Ultimate Guide to Romani Witchcraft, Signs, Symbols, Talismans, Charms, Amulets, Tarot, Spells, and More

Introduction

Gypsies are rightly famous for their psychic powers and unjustly and unfairly infamous for all the wrong things. This book is focused on the specific and wide-ranging magical and psychic abilities that have been passed down for generations of the Romani people. It does not deal with the unjust way the world treats the Romani people or those who do not or did not understand the power of magic and try to fit squares and rectangles into circles and spheres.

The gypsy world is filled with joy and happiness, despite gypsies' relentless struggles to fight for dignity and respect. The Romani people have stood by their own, fought against oppression and unfair discrimination, and come out strong, never letting go of their culture, even as they happily and humbly embraced the culture and religion of the places to which they moved and migrated.

This book gives you an in-depth study of the Romani people, their origins, and their migrations to different geographies. It discusses how they saved their culture, magic, and psychic powers. It gives you amazing insights into symbols and signs that the Romani could read and understand in ways non-Romani could never do.

This book deals with how the gypsies embraced the power of nature and used what Mother Earth gives in abundance to heal themselves and those in need. As they traveled around the world, the Romani picked up valuable lessons and tried to share them with others, even as they used them for their own good. They learned and embraced the connection between humanity and divinity and harnessed divine energy to improve their lives.

Read on to find a detailed, comprehensive guide on gypsy magic and how to use it to enhance the quality and meaning of your life. It is replete with all the information you need to learn and practice gypsy magic. So, go ahead and turn the page.

Chapter 1: Gypsy Witchcraft Basics

For centuries, gypsies have had a mysterious, exotic aura about them—or at least, that is how the non-gypsies view them. They have been nomads for generations, traveling around the globe and having no steady place they call home. Yet, they have an identity, a history, a name for themselves, and roots from ancient times.

For centuries, gypsies have had a mysterious, exotic aura about them.
https://www.pexels.com/photo/a-fortune-telling-session-in-progress-6944915/

There is an old saying among the Romani people that goes like this, "Ki shan i Romani/ Adoi san' i chov'hani," which translates to "Wherever gypsies go, there the witches are, we know." The Romani people, commonly known as gypsies, were nomads or eternal wanderers. Their magical practices and customs relied heavily upon an oral tradition. It is believed that they came to be known as "gypsies" in Europe because the Europeans thought they were from Egypt.

Understanding the Romani People

The Romani people (also referred to as the Roma) were as diverse as the geographies and populations of the world. They were also known by names aligned with their rooted culture. In Spain, they were called Gitanos. In France, they were named "gitan." In Central and Eastern Europe, they were called Tsingani. Across the Scandinavian regions, they were called by different words based on the local language, all of which translates to "traveler."

Interestingly, the Romani people called themselves by different names. In England and Portugal, the Romani called themselves Kale. In France, they called themselves Manush, and in western Europe and Germany, they called themselves Sinti. Regardless of where they lived, the Romani people were collectively called gypsies; a term used to refer to people who migrated all over the world over several centuries. Gypsies are those who never have a permanent home. Here are some intriguing and interesting facts about Romani people.

They originated in India. Based on linguistic analysis, experts believe that the Romani originated in the northern plains of India. Many of the words of the languages they speak are very similar to Hindi, one of the major languages spoken in India, especially in the northern parts of this Asian country.

Genetic evidence also suggests that the Romani have their roots in India. A 2012 study published in the *Journal of Cell Biology* involved collecting and analyzing people from numerous Romani cultures around the world. This study observed that the Romani people likely migrated from India about 1,500 years ago. Present-day European Romani people are believed to have traveled through the Balkans more than 900 years ago.

In India, they were called Doms, which translates to "men". Doms became Roms and then Romani right across Europe. However, in North Africa and the Middle East, they call themselves Doms or Domi.

There are about twelve million Romani people globally. Experts opine that the Romani people left India about 1,500 years ago and mostly traveled to Europe. They are believed to have gone to some Eastern European countries such as Romania and Bulgaria. About twelve percent of the Romani people are found in these regions today. Turkey, Slovakia, Russia, Serbia, Hungary, France, and Spain also have a large Romani population.

While the Romani are found primarily in Europe, many have made other nations their home, too.

- About a million Romani have made the United States their home.
- There are about 800,000 in Brazil.
- Doms have also made many Middle East countries their homes, such as Iran, Cyprus, Lebanon, Syria, Israel, and Jordan.

Horrific discrimination and persecution have fallen upon the Romani people wherever they went. When they first migrated to the continent, the Europeans enslaved them.

Romani enslaved people were prevalent right up to the nineteenth century. Right through the Medieval Ages, the Romani people in Europe were persecuted, punished, and even sentenced to death for the flimsiest reasons, often without a simple trial. For example, in 1554, a law was passed in England that said the sentence for living like a gypsy was death.

Thanks to all the discrimination, persecution, and misplaced fear, the Romani people have been seen as thieving, cunning foreigners who steal and move on to the next place for more thieving. Yet, their power of magic was feared, too.

In Germany, gypsies were imprisoned indiscriminately and forced to do hard labor. After repeated attacks, many surviving gypsies formed violent gangs, initially hoping to protect themselves, but soon turned their violence against everyone.

In 1790, the King of Prussia saw the gypsies as an opportunity and converted it into an advantage both for his kingdom and for the gypsies. He decreed that all gypsy men should enlist in the military: A wise move that was followed by other European kingdoms. Since then, gypsy men have done military service for almost all European nations.

Countless reports of violent acts have been documented against them. For example:
- Romani children were abducted from their homes for slavery and prostitution.
- Women's ears were cut off.
- Hot irons were used to brand gypsies.
- Gypsies were prohibited from following their customs and rituals or speaking their language. Cultural and religious conversions were forced upon them.
- Intermarriage within the Romani community was forbidden.

The persecution of the Romani was at its worst during the Nazi regime. The BBC reported that they were the first targets of Nazi atrocities, followed closely by Jews and homosexuals. An estimated two million Romani are believed to have died in Nazi concentration camps. They were the guinea pigs for all evil Nazi torture and other extermination experiments.

Even today, they face discrimination and persecution and continue to fight for their rights. For example, some countries do not provide housing facilities to the Romani, even to those born in those nations. They end up living in metallic makeshift homes without access to water and sanitation. Some other countries do not hesitate to expel the Romani people.

However, in recent times, multiple Romani organizations have been formed to fight for their rights and stop discrimination and persecution. Further, many organizations have come forward to provide resources for the growth and development of the Romani people, especially through education.

The rich culture of the Romani people has been an inspiration for many musicians worldwide, most notably Franz Liszt, the famous classical composer. Gypsy music has inspired many genres of music, such as bolero, jazz, flamenco, etc.

Music played an important role in the life of the Romani people. The reason for this is quite obvious, considering that at the beginning of their migration from India, the Romani people's professions included music and dance, performances, etc.

Family was paramount among the Romani people. Families with similar dress codes, occupations, and language usually grouped together into "tribes." Each group had its own specific nationality, too.

Considering that they originated in India, the Romani were believed to be originally Hindus. However, they assimilated and adopted the religions of the various lands as they migrated and traveled across the globe. Today, most follow some form of Islam or Christianity, retaining a few of the original Romani customs and traditions.

The Romani People From Around the World

In India, gypsies were considered low-caste people who traveled around the country as singers and musicians. It is believed that in 430 BCE, an Indian king gifted 12,000 people from a low-caste tribe to Bahram V, a Persian King. These people made Persia their home for a while before moving to other parts of the Middle East and Europe. Some could have escaped from slavery, while others were kidnapped and captured by the Byzantines and then found their way into Syria and other Middle Eastern and European countries.

Gypsies traveled far and wide, much more than any other group of people. Their knowledge about the world and the happenings in the world was unparalleled. Therefore, rumors spread that they were used as spies, especially during wars.

European Roma

Most of the Roma in Germany and German-occupied territories in pre-war Europe belong to the Roma and Sinti tribes or family groups. They speak a Sanskrit-based dialect. Some follow Islam, while others are Christians.

In Europe, the term "Roma" includes both the Sinti and Roma tribes. Some of the Roma tribespeople prefer being referred to as "gypsies." Interestingly, in German, *Zigeuner*, which means "untouchable, is the word for gypsy.

The European Roma in pre-war Europe worked as artisans, performers, and craftsmen. They were blacksmiths, toolmakers, horse traders, tinsmiths, circus animal trainers, dancers, etc. There were a few Romani shopkeepers, too, in pre-war Germany. By the early twentieth century, the nomadic lifestyle was on the decline.

Before World War II, the population of Roma in Europe was over one million. Most of the gypsy population was concentrated in and around Eastern European countries, such as the former Soviet Union, Poland, Romania, etc. Western European countries, such as the former Yugoslavia, Bulgaria, Germany, and Hungary, also had a sizable Roma population. Many of the above Roma people faced horrific persecution during the Nazi regime, and their population declined considerably.

Egyptian Doms

As mentioned at the start of this chapter, the word gypsy was coined by Europeans when they mistook travel migrants from northern parts of India to have come from Egypt. However, there are gypsies from Egypt, too, most commonly called Doms, who are believed to have psychic and magical powers.

Today, gypsies found in Eastern Africa, including Egypt, Israel, Turkey, and Syria, are called Doms. Like the Roma in Europe, the Doms are marginalized and persecuted. Doms are not officially recognized in Egypt, thanks to a law connected with the country's national identity card. Only three religions are recognized in Egypt: Islam, Christianity, and Judaism. Anyone following any other religion or ethnicity is not issued a national identity card in Egypt. Therefore, Bedouins, Nubians, and, of course, Doms are not recognized in Egypt, and because of this, there is no official record of their population and related parameters.

The Doms of Egypt are divided into different tribes, including the Halebi, the Ghagar, and the Nawar. Sadly, these words are insults in Arabic. It is believed that Ghagar, which loosely translates to "vagrant," could be the largest Dom group. According to a 50-year-old ethnographic research survey conducted by the late Nabil Sobhi Hanna, the Ghagars lived outside villages, on the edges, as they were not allowed entry inside. They were donkey and horse dealers, entertainers, and ironsmiths.

More recently, they have migrated to Cairo. Unfortunately, most of them resort to begging when the income from dwindling trades is insufficient to meet their survival needs. Interestingly, although Doms now lead sedentary lifestyles, their professions continue to reflect their nomadic spirit. Most of the Doms occupy rented homes and move often. They take up short-term jobs and live on the edge of Egyptian societies.

Doms in the Middle East

In the Middle East, Doms lead a varied lifestyle. Some are still nomadic, lead peripatetic lives, and are entertainers, metal workers, musicians, and migrant workers. They work part-time in fields, especially during harvest seasons when you can see many Doms harvesting crops in the Jordan Valley. They also work in the tobacco fields of northern Jordan. A few Middle Eastern Doms are pastoralists. In Iraq, Doms still move around in their colorful caravans and wear costumes as dancers, fortune tellers, acrobats, jugglers, and musicians.

The Roma and Music

During the nineteenth century, gypsies were recognized for their excellent music skills, especially in Russia, Hungary, and Spain. Gypsy minstrels were an integral part of the Hungarian nobility. Dedicated minstrels played for guests during banquets, feasts, and other celebratory events hosted by Hungarian nobles. Nearly all Hungarian bands of royal families had at least one Romani violin virtuoso.

The Social and Family Life of the Romani People

As mentioned, the Romani hardly followed the social rules of an organized society. And yet, they had their own rules under an umbrella of a social and communal set of regulations called Romano, which governed things like hygiene and cleanliness within the homes, and in the community, respect for everyone, respect for justice, etc. Romano means to act and behave in a dignified manner with everyone.

According to the gypsy rules, they have arranged marriages wherein the groom's father approaches the bride's father to ask her hand in marriage for his son—the right to accept or refuse remains with the young couple. The groom's father had to pay a bride price, the amount of which depended on many factors, including the family's status, history, whether the bride had earning potential, etc.

After the marriage, the bride moves into her husband's house and lives with her in-laws. She is expected to do the household chores and look after her husband and his family's welfare. Many times, daughters are exchanged as brides. Thus, the daughter of one household becomes the daughter-in-law of another household, and the daughter of the second household becomes the daughter-in-law of the first.

The family is the most important unit among the Romani people, considering they have no country, kingdom, or republic to which they belong. Typically, a family consists of the head of the unit, his wife, their sons and daughters-in-law, unmarried adults, children, and grandchildren.

The Romani people also follow a social hierarchy beyond the family. About ten or more extended families—sometimes, the number of families could be as large as a hundred—grouped under a social and community umbrella are referred to as kumpania. Each kumpania travels in caravans as one big group. Within each band, small groups called vistas are formed and connected through common ancestry.

Here are some more interesting facts about the social structure of the Romani people:

- The head of a kumpania was called voivode. He held his position throughout his entire lifetime. The next voivode was elected when the previous one died.
- A post called "phuri dai" within every tribe existed. This post was usually held by a wise, old, and experienced Romani woman. She was in charge of looking after women's and children's issues in the kumpania.
- The display of wealth was considered a matter of pride among the Romani people and was considered honorable. They loved opulence. The women proudly wore ornate headdresses and gold jewelry. Gold and silver coins were used to decorate homes.
- Sharing and being generous with your wealth and resources was considered a matter of pride and honor, and food and drink were lavished on guests.
- Generosity and sharing were considered an ethical, moral investment they could call upon during bad times.

The Romani People, Religion, and Witchcraft

The Romani people do not have a single faith or religion they follow. More often than not, they embrace and adopt the religion of the host country. Therefore, in the Middle East, the Doms are devout Muslims. It is common to see Doms undertake the annual pilgrimage to Mecca.

There are Christian gypsies in many countries who follow various sects of Christianity, such as Anglican, Pentecostal, Baptist, and Catholicism. And yet, for the Doms, religion is very personal. They do not discuss or talk about their faith with people.

They are superstitious—they call it magic—and embrace the good elements of all religions. They are deeply spiritual, and spiritism is dominant in their way of thinking and understanding the world and how it works. They fear curses and evil spirits, and therefore, they are happy to help others ward off evil entities and curses through magic and witchcraft.

Even today, the Romani people fear the "mullo" or the ghost of a dead person. The fear of being haunted is so deep that they destroy everything that belonged to dead people, including their wagons, clothes, etc. By destroying all of these items, they believed that the ghosts of dead people would not have anything to return to and, therefore, would not come back to haunt the living people. In fact, the Roma of England even set fire to the wagon of the dead person.

The first adage mentioned in this chapter translates to "Wherever gypsies go, there the witches are, we know." For generations, the Romani people have made a living through fortune-telling. Interestingly, spices and their smells play a big role in witchcraft. Considering that it is believed that the Roma originated in India, it is no surprise that spices—also found extensively in India from ancient times—play such an important part in their lives and from their lives to their professions, one of which is witchcraft.

Gypsy women were known to be excellent spell casters and practitioners of witchcraft. Settled citizens of the countries they migrated to looked at gypsies with suspicion, considering they were wanderers with no permanent place they called home. Interestingly, not having a permanent place to call home did not dent their confidence and pride. Their primary focus is to live life on their terms. They dislike being bound by rigid societal rules that do not fit in with their culture and belief systems. Although they want the best for their children, they choose not to educate them in a bid to make them less "modern" and more attached to their own culture.

Interestingly, despite all the hardships they face, the gypsies cling to their magic and witchcraft, both of which are deeply integrated into their culture. While doubters and cynics around the world question the "power and sense" in doing magic, for the gypsies, the practice of magic is considered useful and productive. The magic they do and the graces and help they seek from the spirits can be equated with how non-gypsies pray to their gods, seeking some things such as the recovery of a lost love or item, protection against danger, a loving partner, etc.

Gypsies are divided into tribes, each with its own symbols and talismans. Most gypsies have basic powers such as spell casting, brewing potions, mediumship—the ability to connect and commune with the spirit world—and divination. There is nothing unique about magic and psychic powers. All of us are born with it. However, the Romani people are among the few who continue to believe in these inherent powers and work hard to cultivate their innate talents and improve their craft.

The gypsies had varying witchcraft beliefs depending on their geography and culture. For example, in some Romani cultures, horses were considered spiritual animals, and keeping a horse's skull was excellent for preventing evil paranormal spirits from entering your home. Most of the gypsy magic centered around nature, animals, plants, and the divine powers of these living beings.

Belief in the divine power of animals is why the Roma revered and valued their animals and cattle highly. They paid close attention to their animals, talked and interacted with them, listened to them, and tried to connect with their spiritual power. Animals were often part of magic rituals.

What non-gypsies call superstition is what gypsies believe are elements of magic and witchcraft. They use amulets, talismans, knots, and charms to enhance the power of their magical prowess. Magical symbols in gypsy magic include stones, knives, shells, and other natural elements. To reiterate, the Romani people tried to harness the magic from the power of nature.

The Roma Today

In the olden days, gypsies would walk through the streets, seeking hands to read and to foretell the future for those who wished to use their witchcraft services. Of course, payment in cash and/or in kind was the crux of the matter for the gypsies. Today, most of them rely on the Internet for their clients.

Also, today's nomadic Romani people use RVs and cars to move from place to place. Many Romani have also settled down and are not easily distinguishable from non-gypsies. In fact, thanks to the discriminatory attitude of society, some Romani people prefer to hide their roots.

And yet, there is a lot of effort to end discrimination and persecution against innocent Roma. Every year, April 8 is celebrated as the International Day of the Roma and is specifically used to spread awareness and celebrate the Roma culture worldwide.

Chapter 2: Lore, Codes, and Beliefs

The gypsy practices and beliefs are as diverse as the geographical nations in which they live. However, this chapter looks at the folktales and beliefs that are more or less common among all gypsies.

The gypsy practices and beliefs are as diverse as the geographical nations in which they live.
https://www.pexels.com/photo/different-artifacts-on-the-black-table-7189440/

Rromanipé or the Gypsy World View

Rromanipé encompasses the ideas of honor, dignity, and justice. As mentioned, the gypsies do not have a common religion; instead, they follow the faith of the host country. They described themselves as "numerous stars scattered in God's sight." The gypsies believe in karma, an element deeply rooted in Indian philosophy.

Loosely translated, karma can be defined as "spiritual balance" or "what goes around comes around." According to Romani philosophy, there is a constant conflict between the Devil and the divine in every human being. The one who wins this conflict decides how your life turns out.

Another important facet of Rromanipé is respect for elders. They strongly believe that when anyone disrespects elders, the ancestor spirits do not rest until the perpetrator is taught a lesson and disciplined. The Romani addressed their god through various names, including Devlam, Devla, Del, and more, and these words have been part of the Romani language since ancient times.

Devla means "God." For the Roma novice, it is important to distinguish this word from the English word "devil." In the Romani language, the word for devil is "beng." Devla is etymologically related to the Sanskrit word "Dev," which means god.

The Roma believe in a spiritual higher power or energy referred to as "dji." This spiritual energy gets diminished when they spend time outside their community, which is why they hesitate to assimilate with non-Roma people and are highly suspicious of outsiders.

In fact, having a distant gypsy cousin does not mean you will be accepted into the Romani fold. Further, one gypsy might not consider another as part of the family or kampania (or kumpania) if the rules and regulations are not strictly adhered to. The ones who do not follow the laws are ostracized and expelled from the community. The gypsies refer to non-gypsies as "Gorgers."

Another interesting aspect of Romano rules is that everything in this world is categorized as elements that are clean and or marime (dirty). Being or becoming marime or coming in contact with anything marime can cause a lot of pain and harm to the victim. You could get bad luck, become sick, contract a disease, and even die. Many things are considered marime, according to Rromanipé. Some of them are:

- Liquid coming out of our bodies (for example, urine)
- Rodents
- Reptiles
- Anything that touches the ground

Once an item is considered marime, the Romani people avoid all contact with it or at least limit contact with the element. The concept of marime and what elements are "dirty" are instilled into them right from birth. Avoiding "dirty" impacts how gypsies live, act, think, and speak.

Further, if a tangible object is considered marime, the words used to describe or name it are also marime. For example, menstruation is marime. Thus, periods and menses are not discussed, nor are the words used in conversation. The Romani language does not have a word for menstruation or many other marime conditions. They are simply referred to as "things." Sometimes, they are given descriptions such as long things, short things, difficult things, bad things, etc.

While certain conditions, such as menstruation, are marime, people experiencing marime conditions are also given special treatment because they can spread marime. For example, women during their menstruation are kept separate. The same holds for people who are ill. If someone is ill, their things are segregated from the rest of the stuff in the home because the illness—which is considered marime—can spread.

The good thing is that people affected by marime conditions are not spoken of in any negative connotation. This is because the Romani believe that marime can also spread through our thoughts. The power of the mind—especially bad or negative thoughts about the affected person—can attract illness or the marime from menstruating women.

Suppose someone is ill in the house. Not giving sympathy to that person or being spiteful can also bring sickness to you. The negative thoughts in your mind "capture" the illness in your body.

The ideas of the Roma people might seem unscientific and illogical to a novice. However, it is not that they do not know how diseases spread; they are more concerned about why certain conditions are caught by some and not by others. The concept of marime is so deeply ingrained in the Roma psyche that it is believed that you can catch not only diseases but also unfortunate events—such as accidents or broken bones—by associating yourself or thinking badly about the affected person, especially those who do not follow Rromano rules.

This is why outsiders—considered marime—are not easily allowed to be assimilated into the Roma fold. According to Rromano, the most marime people are those who do not follow the code of conduct, cleaning rules, and other Roma rituals, which translates to everything outside the kumpania.

Even washing the dishes is done ritualistically. The order of washing is dependent on the amount of contact the dish has had with the human body. The dishes that come directly in contact with the human body are washed first in the cleanest water. Therefore, cups that touch our lips are washed first—with the purest water—and plates and pots only touched by our hands are washed last. Food from pots is transferred to the plate before it is eaten. A Roma will never take food directly from the pot and put it into their mouth.

Most importantly, dishes must be washed using running water, not stagnant water. Considering all these restrictions and rules, living the life of a nomadic Roma can be quite challenging and stressful. They are always thinking of how to avoid marime and live life according to Rromano, lest they get punished.

Gypsy Lore

Baba Fingo — Legend has it that Baba Fingo was the leader of the Romani people in ancient Egypt. The Roma were persecuted, oppressed, and severely discriminated against by the Pharaoh of Egypt. Baba Fingo led his people to the Red Sea to escape the oppressive regime so that they could hide under the water and be safe from the atrocities of Egyptian soldiers.

The Roma community in Egypt believes that on May 6, every year, Baba Fingo is resurrected, and the day is celebrated as an annual festival called the Kakava Festival, specifically in the northwestern provinces of Turkey. This festival is also connected to the ancient tradition of Hıdırellez, a celebration of the coming of spring. The Roma believe that the Kakava Festival brings blessings and abundance to all the participants.

The Legend of Bibi — Bibijako Djive is one of the most important festivals celebrated by the Romani people following the Eastern Orthodox Christian belief. The faith in Bibi and her legendary powers are connected with the Roma community in Serbia. The celebration of this festival is to appease Bibi, the goddess of cholera, so the Roma children are not affected by the disease. Bibi's legend goes as follows.

According to a paper published by Svetlana M Cirkovic entitled "Bibi and Bibijako Djive in Serbia" in the *Academia Journal*, Kona was an Eastern Orthodox Christian Roma settled in Serbia. She died in 1935 at the age of 99. She is believed to have seen Bibi for the first time. This legend claims that one day on a cold winter evening, when Kona and her family were finishing supper, there was a knock at the door. Kona's husband opened the door to see Bibi standing outside. She was tall, skinny, and bony. She wore a red dress, had long dark hair, and was barefoot. With her were two girls dressed in white and two lambs.

The husband invited them in and told Bibi she seemed very tired and asked her to sit down and relax. He also asked her if she was hungry. Bibi asked the family for a pair of peasant shoes because she was barefoot. Kona found a pair and gave it to Bibi.

The instant Kona gave the pair of peasant shoes to Bibi, she, along with the children and the lambs, vanished into thin air. The main door remained shut, and Kona's family heard Bibi's voice saying, "May God always give you and your family everything you need."

The surprised couple opened the door and went outside, hoping to see Bibi. However, she was knocking on the neighbor's door, a wealthy Serbian household. The rich Serbian woman opened the door and chased Bibi away rudely. Bibi cursed the rich family and returned to Kona's home, where she decided to spend the night with her two children and the lambs.

After being fed and warmed, Bibi put her children to sleep and said to Kona, "I am Cholera, and I have suffocated the children of your rich but rude neighbor. Celebrate my feast every year and make an inscription (Zapis) for my children on that day. Shout out loud the following verse, 'To the health of the Aunt and her children.'"

The family then turned in for the night. When they woke up the next morning, Bibi and her children were not found anywhere. Suddenly, loud wails were heard from the neighbor's house. When Kona and her husband went to see what happened, they realized the children of the rich household were all dead. From that day onward, the Roma celebrate Bibi and her children.

In Serbia, the word for aunt is *Tetka*. When the Romani people adopted the divine Aunt into their worship, they christened her Bibi, which is Aunt in the Romani language. The Roma now believe that the children of those who do not celebrate Bibi on that day—as ordained by her—are cursed to die.

Gypsy lore is filled with miracles and dreams involving Bibi. The Romani people believe that if Bibi came in their dreams, she would usually ask for a certain task to be completed concerning her feast or the way she expected to be honored. Sometimes, she would appear in the dreams of those who did not celebrate her feast. The Romani people's faith in Bibi and her miraculous powers is legendary.

Dhampirs — Dhampirs are protectors and guardians, specifically for the protection of the Moroi, an ancient, magical race of benevolent vampires with fangs that feed on blood. The Moroi do not wear capes, sleep in coffins, or turn into bats. They don't like the daylight like the maleficent vampires. However, the Moroi are not eternal and do not need humans to survive.

Dhampirs are part-Moroi and part-human and are dedicated to protecting the Moroi from their monstrous, deadly counterparts, the Strigoi. Dhampirs are born with excellent reflexes, amazing agility, increased strength and power, and outstanding endurance.

Today, dhampirs are famous in entertainment as they are included in multiple fantasy films and books. However, the idea of dhampirs is rooted in gypsy folklore. It is the name given to the child of a vampire by the Slavonic gypsies. According to gypsy lore, the child has a few vampire powers. The story of how dhampirs are born is also found in gypsy lore.

It is believed that when a new vampire wakes up, he is extremely aroused. Since he is new and has not yet found a vampire mate, he goes in search of the widow he has left behind in the human world to satiate his sexual desires. If he does not have a widow for this purpose, he just finds any young woman.

The widow or the young woman can get impregnated by the new vampire, and the baby born out of this union is a dhampir. The gypsies had other names for this being. The female of this species was called Vampira, and the male was Vampir. While there were varying beliefs about the kind of powers this special child had, there was no doubt that a human with vampire blood got superpowers in some form. Some of them craved blood, while others did not need it. The Serbian gypsies believed that vampires were invisible to humans, but dhampirs could see them.

Ursitory — The Ursitory is known by many names, including Urmen, Ursoni, Ourmes, Oursitori, etc. They are a group of three female spirits (or fairies) of fate or destiny. According to Romani folklore, the three fate spirits appear three nights after the birth of a child to decide their fate. The benevolent or good fairy foresees happy, bright future events for the child. The sad, pessimistic spirit foresees the worst things happening in the child's future.

The third one, the most powerful fairy, is the impartial one dedicated to sensibility and reason. She settles the child's fate after taking input from the good and the bad fairies. Her decision on the child's fate is binding, and once the fate is sealed by the Urmen, no one and nothing can change it.

Vampire Pumpkins and Watermelons — This legend originated from the Romani people in the Balkans in southeast Europe. The Romani people believe that watermelons and pumpkins have special properties. These two vegetables can acquire vampire traits if left out the entire night under the full moon's effects. The first and most obvious sign of vampirism is a drop of blood that can be seen on the rind of these vegetables.

The Roma believe that only pumpkins—all kinds of pumpkins—and watermelons have the power to transform into vampires. While some believe the transformation happens during a full moon night, others believe the vegetables turn into vampires when they fight each other.

When the pumpkins and/or watermelons are kept together for more than ten days, they begin to come alive, stir themselves up, and make growling sounds. The vampire vegetables and normal ones look alike, and it is impossible to discern differences except for the drop of blood on the vampires.

The vampire vegetables are believed to roam around the villages and gypsy caravans at night. However, they are believed to be harmless to people. Thus, most gypsies are not scared of vampire pumpkins and watermelons.

The codes, beliefs, and magical creatures and beings discussed in this chapter—there are many, many more—are why gypsies are scared of the power of sinister magic. Their belief is genuine, and just because non-gypsies don't understand it doesn't give them a right to mock or disrespect gypsy lore, codes, and beliefs.

Chapter 3: Gypsy Omens and Customs

The Romani often look at the weather and the nature around them for omens that may predict what may happen in the near or far future. Let us look at some of these elements and omens and understand how gypsies read and interpret their meanings.

The Romani often look at the weather and the nature around them for omens that may predict what may happen in the near or far future.
https://www.pexels.com/photo/a-person-covering-the-lighted-candle-he-is-holding-5435272/

Weather and Sky Omens

Gypsies try to read and interpret the meanings of weather, climate, and the sky above. They try to understand why and how weather and climate change, why the colors of the sky change, how the rain falls, etc.

While the modern world has scientific explanations for many natural occurrences today, the belief system followed by the gypsies can also be connected with these scientific reasons in small but certain ways. When we find this connection, it is easy to understand the working of a gypsy magician's mind. So, let us get to these elements and their meanings.

Rain

Rain is perhaps one of the most relaxing events that bring peace and happiness to most of us. Sitting at the window and listening to raindrops patter on our roofs and trees is so calming.

According to gypsies, rain symbolizes good luck, clarity, and cleansing. This is true because when it rains, all the muck and dirt on the earth is taken away by the rainwater into streams, ponds, and rivers, allowing Mother Nature to work on them and convert them into fertile soil and fertilizers.

Therefore, rain cleanses the pollution and dirt physically. Rain stands for cathartic cleansing as well. It is seen as a redeeming event, allowing us to clear our minds of negative and bad thoughts and lighten the burden of our overburdened souls.

Rain is also a symbol of calmness and clarity. Even when it storms, it stands for this meaning. This is because when there is a storm, we are all forced to retreat indoors, and we get the time to relax and look inward, which helps us calm down. The sound of rain is often like a lyrical, rhythmic lullaby lulling us to restful sleep.

You can speak to any farmer, and their first love is almost always rain! When it rains, crops and plants flourish, creating more food, wood, and many other survival elements and natural beauty, greenery, and other harbingers of joy and happiness for human beings. More often than not, the coming of rain and monsoons heralds a cleansing period and oncoming good fortune.

Rain also symbolizes rebirth and growth. It keeps the cycle of life going while helping plant life flourish and grow. Water is the symbol of life, and rain represents this powerful symbol. Without rain or water, life would not exist on Earth! And this is why rains are seen as bountiful and beneficial in the Romani belief system. So, if it rains on your wedding day, your married life will be filled with good fortune, abundance, and happiness.

Mist

Mist is commonly believed to be a mediator between the known and the unknown. It is believed to connect reality with non-reality elements such as dreams, illusions, divination, apparitions, etc. The Roma believe that early morning mist signals a good day ahead. For winter, it means the coming of more cold weather and wind.

Other Weather-Related Omens

The following signs foretell rain:
- If the sky has the color of a mackerel.
- If the sky has a greenish tinge.
- If you see a haloed moon or froth along the edges of a body of water.
- If you see a meat-eating animal like a dog or cat consuming grass or a cat scratching itself against the legs of a table.
- If you see snails in the twilight or the sounds of crickets are louder than usual.
- When you see cattle or cows lying down early in the morning.
- When you see swallows flying low.
- When fowl and/or peacocks call or sing.
- When you see rooks circling in the sky.
- When robins perched in low branches sing.
- When you see seagulls on land.
- When a rooster alights on a gate and crows.
- When you see mist high on the hills.
- When chimney smoke falls instead of rising, a storm is expected.

Other signs:
- When snow lingers in a place, more snow will fall.
- When it rains heavily in September, there will be a drought.
- When your fireplace is burning well with many sparks, cold weather is coming.

- When you see numerous hawberries, the upcoming winter will be cold and bitter.
- When you rub a cat and see sparks on its fur, cold weather is coming.
- When a cricket chirps inside the house, a cold winter will follow.
- When a blown-out candle flame smolders for a long time, the oncoming winter will be bad.

Mild winters or good weather can be expected:

- When the ticking of watches is loud before the onset of winter.
- When spiders spin cobwebs on the grass.
- When there is little or no smoldering when a candle is blown out, fair weather can be expected.

For weather-related omens, Fridays and Mondays have some connection with gypsy lore. If there is a storm on Friday, there will also be a storm on Monday. Or if the sunset on Friday is splendorous, it will rain on Monday. A warm October means a cold February.

Animal Omens

Animals and plants are deeply connected to the Romani way of life. They read and interpret animal behavior and sounds in different ways.

Here are some interesting weather beliefs based on animal omens:

- If you see a cat washing its ears, good weather can be expected.
- An old, weak cat dancing around unusually could mean the onset of windy weather.
- If a dog howls without reason, it signals an impending death.
- The Romani people regard Foxes as lucky omens, and their behavior toward you could bring a little or lots of good luck. For example, a good opportunity might come your way if you encounter a fox while traveling. If this fox gazes at you for a while, it is an extremely good omen.
- The sight of a mule shaking itself is a sign of good luck.
- The sight of a moth hovering near a flame signifies upcoming good news.
- Seeing a white horse early in the morning means good luck will be with you throughout the day.

- Two horses playing together means happiness and joy in the family. However, if two horses are fighting, squabbles and fights can be expected in the family.
- If you see a crow standing on the road, your journey will be happy and/or fruitful.
- If a gypsy sees a dead crow on the road, they will turn back.
- Rooks are seen as harbingers of bad luck. However, if you have a property with a well-established rookery, it is a good sign. If the rooks leave after you buy the property, it is considered a bad sign or an upcoming calamity. Imagine buying a property with a rookery in Ireland, and suppose the rooks leave the nests within the year; you have the right to take back your money and return the property to the owner.
- If you see two magpies together, it is a good sign. However, if you see only one, it signals that a theft is in the offing.
- Flying wrens and robins bring good luck, while dead ones herald bad luck.
- If you hear an owl or try to capture or kill one during the day, it is an ill-omen. If an owl hoots very close to dawn, it calls for a human's soul and signals death.
- Seagulls flying over a gypsy wagon are considered an ill-omen, which means the death of someone in the family.

Other Common Beliefs and Omens of the Romani People

According to the Romani people, money and itching have a connection. If your right palm itches, you will receive an income, or someone will give you money. If your left palm itches, there is an impending expenditure, or you will give away money. If you put your handbag on the floor, it is believed that you will lose money.

Another money omen is this: Gypsies do not count currency notes in fours because it brings bad luck; they only count in threes as this brings good fortune.

If your nose itches, there are several connotations. One is that someone could slap you. An itching nose when someone is talking could mean the talker is lying. Itching feet could indicate impending travel.

Itching in the right eye is a sign of ill luck, whereas if your left eye itches, something good will happen.

Bad luck omens — It is common to forget something while leaving home. Most of us would go back and pick up what we forgot. For a Roma, though, this will never happen because going back home after leaving the house for some task brings bad luck. So, the best thing is to manage the day without the thing you forgot or postponing the task for another day.

Red and white flowers represent blood and the gut. Placing these two flowers brings bad luck. Cutting nails on a Sunday brings bad luck. Burning flour or bread is considered an ill omen.

Umbrella omen — Opening an umbrella inside the house is irrational for the Roma and a sign of bad luck. Therefore, a Roma will never open their umbrella inside the house.

Omens heralding family fights — Spilling salt on the dining table is a definite sign of an impending fight or argument in the family.

Hiccups and omens — If you are hiccupping without a break and reason, it could mean that someone is thinking of you. If you can guess the person thinking of you, the hiccupping will stop.

Black cat omen — If a black cat crosses your path, turn around and find another way to reach your destination because, according to the Romani people, a black cat is a sign of bad luck.

Sharing bottle omen — The Romani people believe that sharing a bottle with friends or family is not a great idea because of the following belief: If you share a bottle of water, juice, or alcohol, you must have the last sip; otherwise, the other person is likely to steal your loved one.

Glass pieces omen — If you are a Roma, breaking glass might not be a bad idea. In some Romani weddings, the bride and groom each throw a glass on the floor. The more the number of pieces the glasses break into, the happier their marriage will be.

Shoe omens — Placing a pair of shoes on the table will attract bad luck. A pregnant woman should never wear new shoes because it is believed that both she and her baby will be put in a coffin! Therefore, the Romani people make sure someone who is not pregnant wears the new shoes first, and then the pregnant lady can wear them.

Other beliefs:
- It is considered ill luck for a woman whose ears are not pierced to have a baby.

- A newborn baby's hair is not cut until their second birthday.
- If you see a shooting star, it is a sign of impending death.
- When a tree is about to die, it is believed to "scream in pain." These screams should not be heard; therefore, gypsies cover their ears with their hands.
- If you see a woman carrying a jug of water, it is good luck. However, if the jug is empty, it is bad luck.
- Slicing an apple in half without cutting the seed means that person's affairs and wishes of the heart will be fulfilled.
- When two people utter the same word or phrase simultaneously, they must link their fingers and make a wish. If they do this, their wishes will come true.

Interpretations of Dreams among Gypsies

Dreams have long been believed to be the voice of the divine trying to send us messages. Gypsies follow their dreams and try to interpret them in many ways.

Here are some pointers on their beliefs on dreams.

- If you dream of bulls, snakes, cats, or knives, it is a sign of bad luck.
- A mule or white horse in your dream means good luck. Dreams of horses mean you will get some news.
- If you see a fire in your dreams, there will be a summons for you.
- If you see a big house in your dream, you could be jailed or arrested.
- If you see people or dogs quarreling in your dream, friends are coming over.
- If you see fish swimming, there will be a scandal.
- Your dreams during the autumn season will come true. If you can recall your dream(s) in the morning, they, too, will come true.

Omens about Days of the Week

The seven days of the week have different meanings and significance to gypsies. Some activities are disallowed on certain days of the week, while some can be done only on certain days. Let us look at some of these

omens in gypsy lore.
- Sowing flax and using scissors and needles are forbidden on Wednesdays and Fridays.
- No bargain or sale can be concluded on Fridays.
- Washing anything on Saturdays and spinning on Thursdays is considered bad luck.

The Romani people always offer flowers to people they meet on the road as they travel. This custom comes from their nomad legacy. As the Romani people traveled from place to place, they offered flowers to strangers they crossed paths with as a gesture of goodwill and a sign of peace. The gypsies strongly believed the Earth was round and that what goes around comes around. That the Earth was round was also the basis for another thought process: If they stay too long in one place, the Earth becomes heavy; if they stay in one place for a short length of time, the Earth becomes light. Thus, the balance of the Earth would be impacted negatively. This is why gypsies do not stay for very long in one place and prefer moving. Therefore, traveling is the way of life for gypsies.

Chapter 4: Signs and Symbols

Since ancient times, human beings have used symbols to communicate and convey messages, much before the advent of written scripts. In fact, the power of a single symbol often can beat the wordy descriptions in an entire book. Symbols and signs are visual shortcuts to the subconscious mind, bringing forgotten memories to the conscious mind.

For example, if you see the symbol of McDonald's, many ideas and thoughts automatically rise to the surface. You could decide you are hungry and want to eat a burger. You could recall something funny or embarrassing that happened to you when you were eating a burger. You could associate people in your life connected with the burger or food. You could remember happy or horrifying sights you saw while chomping on your burger. The thing here is that without a single word being spoken, the lone sign conjures images and memories in our minds. That is the power of a sign or symbol.

This chapter discusses some of the most important gypsy symbols used in witchcraft practices.

Amulets and Talismans

Many gypsies carry talismans and amulets as good luck and protection charms. According to Romani's belief, an amulet is an item found in nature that is naturally empowered with magic. An amulet can also be artificially empowered—through rituals—with magic.

Talismans are not found in nature. They are human-made and charged with magic by gypsy witches or sorcerers. Typically, a talisman would be a coin or parchment paper inscribed with powerful magical words and/or symbols.

Gypsies carry their talismans and amulets in a leather or cloth pouch called "parik-til" or "putsi," which is normally hung around their necks. To the novice, this little pouch might seem nothing more than a decorative item. However, it is important not to be fooled because this little "putsi" could be filled with magical items.

The important thing about charms, whether amulets or talismans, is to keep them close for the magic to be effective in your life. If you find one or someone gives you one, do not put it away and forget about it. You can keep it in your purse or pocket, or make a small piece of jewelry with it, like a necklace or bracelet, and wear it on your body. Even during rituals, gypsies ensure that they keep protective and good luck charms that are used to enhance the power of the rituals close by.

Horseshoe

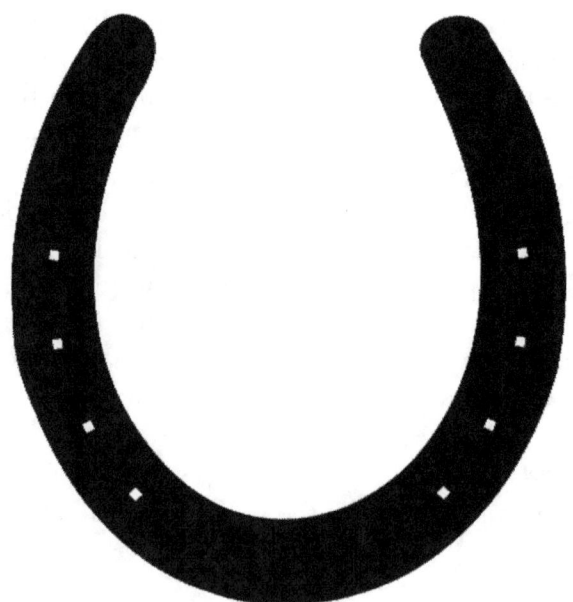

Horseshoe.
https://pixabay.com/es/vectors/herradura-silueta-suerte-negro-306844/

For gypsies, a horseshoe is a symbol of good luck and protection. All their horse-drawn wagons (*vardo*) will have a horseshoe tied to them for protection against evil spirits and for good luck. Gypsy women wear gold or silver horseshoe-shaped talismans around their necks for the same reason.

If gypsies find an abandoned horseshoe with its nails still intact, it will bring luck to the finder for an entire year. However, if it's found facing upwards, it signifies extremely bad luck. It's spat upon and thrown over the finder's left shoulder to prevent the ill luck from affecting the finder's life.

There is an interesting story about how gypsies came to believe that horseshoes bring good luck. Here is how the story goes. Once upon a time, there lived four demons: Death, Ill-Health, Bad Luck, and Unhappiness. One day, these four demons chased a gypsy on horseback. Bad Luck was swifter than the others, so he began to close the gap between himself and the hapless gypsy.

Suddenly, the gypsy's horse threw a shoe at Bad Luck, and he died instantly. The three brothers had to stop and bury their dead brother. The gypsy took the horseshoe home, and the three brothers plotted revenge against the gypsy. But the horseshoe continued to keep gypsies safe from the three vengeful brothers.

The Vardo is the most important possession of gypsies; therefore, a horseshoe is always hung over the door for protection. The vardos are all beautifully and colorfully hand-painted by the owners. The doorways are almost always exquisitely decorated, and the most gorgeous hand-painted horseshoes are hung over them. Horseshoes are used in weddings for the welfare and protection of the bride, groom, and their marriage.

Here's another legend from the Christian world explaining the good luck omen of horseshoes. There lived a farrier (someone who shoes horses) called Dunstan in the tenth century. One day, when he was shoeing a horse alone in his smithy, the Devil came along and wanted cloven hooves for himself. The Devil thought he would be able to travel far and wide comfortably as animals do with cloven hooves.

Dunstan agreed to the Devil's request but decided to help humanity with this act. Dunstan put the nails too close to where the hooves meet the skin, and the Devil cried out in agony. Then, Dunstan made a bargain with the Devil. Dunstan extracted a promise from the Devil that evil would not enter those homes with a horseshoe hanging outside the door. Only when the Devil made this promise did Dunstan remove the painful nails. Since then, people have used horseshoes to keep out ill luck.

Horse Brasses

Horse Brass.
https://commons.wikimedia.org/wiki/File:Horsebrass.jpg

The horse brass is an important gypsy talisman. Horse brasses are one or more symbols made from brass and hung from the horse's harness. Sometimes, many such horse brass plates are strung together on something called a martingale, which looks like a belt or strip of leather hanging from a gypsy's belt. These horse brasses were originally used to protect the animals from the evil eye and diseases and were also worn by people for strength, endurance, and fertility.

The symbols used for horse brasses include many elements from ancient times to modern-day belief systems, including stars, sun, moon, crosses, the three-legged sun wheel (or triskele), bells, images or plates cut in the shape of a horse, acorns, etc. Some designs have a heart at the base, symbolizing "giving heart" to the horse for increased strength.

The Hamsa and the Evil Eye

The Hamsa.
https://pixabay.com/es/illustrations/mano-de-f%c3%a1tima-hamsa-khamsa-3408067/

Evil Eye.
https://www.pexels.com/photo/a-blue-hanging-ornament-12133992/

The evil eye is a particular kind of magical curse believed to harm the targeted person(s) in the form of ill health, bad luck, and even death. Nearly all of us are targets of the evil eye or the dirty look, and most simply shrug it off as mere superstition. However, for the Romani people and many cultures around the globe, the evil eye concept is taken very seriously. Gypsies treat it as an extremely harmful malady that needs to be gotten ridden or taken care of immediately.

So, what is the evil eye? It is the evil look of someone intended to cause harm to the targeted person supernaturally. The evil eye can be in the form of a dirty look toward the target's good fortune, abundance, health, good looks, or anything that can invoke jealousy. It can also take the form of unguarded comments about the target and their good life. The health-related evil eye effects usually come in the form of fatigue, insomnia, diarrhea, and depression.

Gypsies, along with many other cultures worldwide, believe that diseases and sickness are rooted in medical issues and magic-related issues. A person can succumb to a malady not just because of a virus but also because of someone's evil eye attack. In fact, even objects can be attacked by an evil eye, which could result in the destruction or repair of the objects. This is the reason why evil eye protective talismans are hung over vardos.

The evil eye history is long and ancient. The gypsies have traveled all over the world, picked up all the elements across cultures and geographies, and used their lessons to protect themselves and their loved ones from the negative effects of the evil eye. The Hamsa is one such protective measure.

The Hamsa in the Hebrew language means "five." It's a beautiful, ubiquitous symbol holding different meanings for different cultures. It's often worn as jewelry. The Hamsa symbol is an upright palm with two thumbs facing opposite directions and three fingers between the two thumbs facing upward. The middle of the palm has a striking eye connected to the five fingers through different lines and twirls.

The Hamsa is known by different names, some of which are discussed below:

- **Hand of Miriam** — Miriam was the sister of Moses, one of the most prominent figures in Biblical history, the man who led his people out of Egyptian captivity and slavery.

- **Hand of Mother Mary** — The Christians call the Hamsa by this name, honoring the revered Mother of Jesus Christ.
- **Hand of Fatima** — The followers of Islam call the Hamsa by this name. Fatima, Prophet Mohammed's daughter, discovered her husband had taken another wife. She got this information while she was cooking. She became upset and dropped the stirrer into the cooking pot but continued to stir the steaming hot contents with her hand. Therefore, this hand became a symbol of fidelity.

When the Hamsa Hand faces downward, it signifies receiving, giving, and welcoming. In this position, the Hamsa represents abundance and good luck. It symbolizes welcoming good things into our lives, including good health, fortune and wealth, and happiness.

The Hamsa facing upward is a sign of protection. Wearing in this position protects the wearer from all kinds of harm and negativity. It also helps the wearer deal with negative emotions, such as worries, fears, insecurities, hatred, etc.

The eye in the middle of the Hamsa offers protection against the evil eye. Sometimes, the Hamsa hand has a lotus instead of the eye in the middle. The lotus stands for purity, regeneration, rebirth, and enlightenment. The fish on the three middle fingers are also for evil eye protection because fish living underwater are never directly visible to the naked eye and, therefore, free from the effects of the evil eye.

The Four-Leaf Clover

The Four-Leaf Clover.
https://pixabay.com/es/vectors/hoja-tr%c3%a9bol-de-cuatro-hojas-152047/

The four-leaf clover is considered an extremely lucky omen by the gypsies. A shamrock is a three-leaf clover often confused with a four-leaf clover. To put things in perspective, for every 10,000 shamrocks, there is one four-leaf clover—and the rarity is what makes it precious and lucky.

The four-leaf clover stands for love, luck, and hope. There is a common saying, "the luck of the Irish," and the reason for this is rooted in the four-leaf clover. Ireland is believed to have far more four-leaf clovers than any other place in the world.

The fourth leaf can be discerned easily because it is of a different green than the other three. If you find a four-leaf clover, it's a sign of good luck. However, if you give away this leaf to someone else, you could get luckier than if you had kept it for yourself. Multiple legends connect the four-leaf clover to good luck. Some of them are detailed below:

- The association of luck with the rare clover is believed to be directly connected with Eve, the first woman, according to Christianity. After being banished from the Garden of Eden, Eve is believed to have picked one four-leaf clover for herself before she left.

- According to Celtic beliefs, four-leaf clovers have magical powers of protection and can ward off bad luck and negative energies. The Celts also believed that if you carried a four-leaf clover, fairies—usually invisible and dangerous little creatures that can harm children—become visible, helping the wearer take protective measures.

- It's also believed that when Saint Patrick brought Christianity to ancient Ireland, he used the three-leaf clover to explain the concept of the Trinity: The Father, the Son, and the Holy Spirit. However, it's possible that Ireland—remember, it's the place where most four-leaf clovers are found—might already have associated magic and magical powers with this rare plant. The old and the new belief systems combined and enhanced the magical power of the four-leaf clover in Ireland.

One interesting final point about four-leaf clovers: If you find one, you are sure to find a few more in the same vicinity. So, do not stop with the luck of one four-leaf clover. Look around and multiply your luck by finding more.

Lucky Penny

Lucky Penny.
https://www.pexels.com/photo/silver-liberty-in-god-we-trust-1978-coin-64824/

The Romani people never leave a penny when they find one on the path they are traveling or anywhere else. The good fortune of a penny is not connected to its value but to the fact that it is made with metal, a scarce element, especially in ancient times compared to now.

Therefore, when someone found a penny, it was believed that it was a gift from God and that the finder would be protected against bad luck. The belief that metal is lucky is also one of the reasons why horseshoes are considered lucky. Finding a penny with its tail side up is considered bad luck in some cultures.

The Irish spit on a penny and throw it into the bushes so that they can be found by mischievous fairies and leprechauns and will give the person good luck. Another belief is that if you find a penny whose year stamp matches your birth year, your luck will be multiplied.

While you can buy good luck amulets and talismans from online and brick-and-mortar shops near you, it's even better if you can make them yourself. Use creativity to beautify your charms and wear them or carry them around to harness their power. Most importantly, when you make amulets and talismans, you transfer your powers and energies into them, customizing and personalizing them for your needs.

The next chapter teaches you the different kinds of amulets and talismans you can create at home.

Chapter 5: How to Make Amulets and Talismans

Just like wandering, nomadic gypsies, anyone who wishes to practice gypsy magic can learn how to create their own talismans and charms from scratch using easily accessible items they can find at home or in budget-friendly stores.

The word amulet comes from the Greek word "amuletum."
https://www.pexels.com/photo/glass-amulets-hanging-on-tree-6243236/

Differences between Amulets and Talismans

Before moving on to making amulets and talismans, let us learn how to distinguish between them. Both are magically charged with spiritual and/or magical power to protect against evil or bring good luck.

The word amulet comes from the Greek word "amuletum," while talisman comes from "telesma," which means "consecration ceremony."

Amulets have the power to ward off negative and evil energy. They either absorb or reflect negative energy targeted at the wearer. Horseshoes, coal, garlic, coins, crucifixes, etc., are some of the amulets people wear for this purpose. Amulets are magical objects that keep the person safe or bring good fortune to the wearer or holder.

Talismans, on the other hand, empower the wearer with positive energy so that negativity does not affect him or her. They are human-made objects charged with magical energy by gypsy magicians or talisman makers. Examples of famous talismans include Aladdin's magic lamp and King Arthur's Excalibur. Magic hats or rods carried by practicing magicians, etc., are also considered talismans.

These magical objects are worn or carried on the person to enhance the wearer or carrier's personal power. Therefore, talismans are amplifiers of a person's personal and magical powers. They guide the wearer to have the right thoughts. They need intense focus and should be crafted in specific periods and rituals.

Often, talismans are made of gemstones and crystals. They are usually a single piece, such as a pendant or a stone fixed on one's bracelet. Conversely, amulets can be simple bags filled with herbs, stones, and other magical objects. Amulets come in their natural form—though they could be magically and energetically empowered through rituals—while talismans are human-made objects.

Colors and Candles in Gypsy Magic

Different colors have different meanings and interpretations in gypsy magic. You can use this section on colors for all your rituals and gypsy magic practice, including making amulets and talismans. Candles are essential items in a gypsy's magical tool kit. They amplify and release the energy needed during and after rituals. You can use colored candles without lighting them for positive vibes and light them in rituals.

Black — Black stands for mystery and protection. It is the color of the clergy. Witches wear black to cloak themselves against evil and to protect their mysteries. It's used for psychic protection. Moreover, it's an all-purpose color—more so in black magic—and can be used for hexing, gathering information, learning new things, wisdom, shapeshifting, scrying, and more.

White — White stands for peace and serenity and promotes insight and personal strength. This is also an all-purpose color in white magic and can be used in rituals involving strength, peace, purity, unity, truth, young children, and balance.

Green — Green stands for growth and development and is great to use when you need your ideas to come alive. It is the color of life, prosperity, money, acceptance, weather, plant magic, and abundance.

Blue — Blue is great for emotional healing and for balancing the chakras. It is the color of communication, good fortune, willpower, concentration, organization, and sincerity, and it stands for the water element.

Yellow — Yellow is great for rituals involving building social and networking skills. It is also good for job opportunities and career growth. It's the color of happiness, success, memory, inspiration, magical practices relating to the Sun, and flexibility.

Red — Red is the color of love, sex, and passion. It stands for sexual potency, courage, danger, action, war, competition, and assertiveness.

Pink — Pink is for romance. Light a pink candle every day at your altar if you want to attract love. It is the color of compassion, femininity, maturity, domestic harmony, and spiritual and emotional healing.

Purple — Purple is the color for creativity and spiritual enlightenment. It works for rituals dealing with wisdom, spiritual power, independence, government-related works, and connecting with the spirits.

Orange — Orange boosts your ambitions and widens your horizons. It is the color of intellectual matters, self-expression, curing addictions, vitality, celebrations, and investments.

Brown — Brown is the color associated with all kinds of resources, especially materialistic resources. It is the color of pet/animal magic, earth, stability, finding lost things, real estate and construction, and food.

Essential Oils in Gypsy Magic

Essential oils are organic compounds extracted from plants and plant parts, such as bark, leaves, flowers, seeds, fruits, and roots. Essential oils have excellent healing and magical properties. They can heal the body, mind, and spirit and have been used for millennia to treat spiritual, mental, and physical illnesses.

Our olfactory system, which deals with our nose and smelling senses, connects these smells to the amygdala, the center of the brain that deals with emotions. It also connects to the limbic system that is responsible for our memories, stress-related issues, breathing, blood pressure, hormone balance, etc.

The above information is known to us through scientific studies in the modern world. However, the wise gypsies of yore already knew about this and used essential oils in their magical practices to harness their powers and magical energies. Here is a list of some essential oils commonly used in gypsy magical practices, such as rituals and making amulets and talismans.

Basil — Gives clarity and mental strength while stimulating the mind. As you breathe in the smell of basil essential oil, your powers of concentration get a big boost, too.

Bergamot — Uplifts you emotionally while soothing and calming your anxiety and feelings of depression. It is great to treat stress, grief, and fear.

Black pepper — Builds mental stamina and enhances the alertness of your mind.

Cinnamon — Great to use during times of worry and fatigue. Stimulates and energizes you.

Clove — Reduces mental exhaustion, anxiety, and depression and relieves stress. It is also known as a great aphrodisiac and is often used to treat insomnia.

Cypress — Aids in focus and concentration and relieves stress.

Eucalyptus — Soothes and calms the body, which is why people often use a few drops of eucalyptus oil in their baths. It stimulates the mind and helps to improve concentration.

Frankincense — Helps to slow down and deepen your breathing and is often used during meditation sessions. It grounds and calms you without any sedative effects.

Jasmine — Soothes the nerves, thereby building self-confidence and optimism. It is great for revitalizing and restoring energy levels. Jasmine is also often used as an aphrodisiac.

Lavender — Very well known for its sedative properties and soothes and calms the mind. It promotes sleep and reduces anxiety and worry.

Lemongrass — Refreshing and uplifting, it spreads happiness in the atmosphere. It combats nerve exhaustion and revitalizes the body and mind.

Myrrh — Helps mellow out heightened emotions and is a great meditation aid. It creates an uplifting and relaxing atmosphere.

Nutmeg — Removes doubt and resistance while improving spontaneity and flexibility.

Orange — Its sunny, positive vibes bring happiness and warmth. It helps to release negativity from your body and mind.

Patchouli — The smell is calming, grounding, and balancing. It gets rid of lethargy while sharpening your wit. It is great for meditation and prayer.

Rose — Aids self-care and self-nurturing by harmonizing the body, mind, and spirit. It helps you build self-esteem and aids in solving your emotional problems. Rose is also an aphrodisiac.

Sage — Commonly used for spiritual purification and cleansing. It helps us adapt to changes by bringing comfort and protection.

Sandalwood — The smell instills a deep sense of inner peace. It has been used in spiritual and magical practices since ancient times.

Vetiver — Helps eliminate anger, resentment, tension, and irritability. It also helps in grounding and is great for meditation sessions.

Ylang-ylang — Sedates the central nervous system, thereby reducing stress and anxiety. It helps us feel happy and grateful for life and what it offers.

How to Create a Simple Gypsy Good Luck Charm or Spell

As explained in the previous chapter, making amulets and talismans is better than purchasing them at a store. So, here is how you can create these easily using the methods given below.

Good Luck Charm with Paper

This is one of the simplest amulets that you can make for yourself. It is flexible enough to be used for any end purpose.

Materials Needed:
- Pens, different colored inks, and/or paint
- Paper
- Essential oils

- Candles

The use of essential oils is optional; however, they have magical perfumery powers that can enhance the amulet's energy. You already know how various symbols and signs are connected with good luck. Having these signs in your home or carrying them on your person will help draw cosmic energies to attract good luck into your life. Creating a good luck scroll with the above materials is one of the easiest ways to do this. Follow this process to make your good luck charm.

- First, cut a small rectangular piece of paper measuring about 4 inches by 3 inches.
- Mark the middle of the cut paper with the symbol of your choice using colored pens, inks, or paint. Remember to use pens with free-flowing inks, such as gel pens, fountain pens, etc.
- Next, write a small phrase or a few words describing your desire at the top or bottom of the paper. Then, add your full name, birth date, and other data that connect you to the paper.
- Now, roll up the scroll and use candle wax to seal it.
- You can anoint the scroll with your preferred choice of essential oil(s). For example, orange, nutmeg, violet, or rose are all excellent for good luck.
- Carry this scroll whenever you want to attract good luck.

What you write on the paper scroll becomes the power of the scroll. Examples of what your good luck scroll could contain include:

- I want a better-paying job.
- I want to attract love into my life.
- I want my ex to come back to me.
- I want to get into a particular university or course.

As you write on the scroll, repeat the intent as many times as you can so that the power is transferred to the scroll and it attracts cosmic energies aligned with this intent.

How to Make a Gypsy Mojo Bag

A gypsy mojo bag called parik-til was introduced in a previous chapter. You can make your parik-til for any intended purpose using a string pouch of any color of your choice, but use the color that is aligned with the purpose of the mojo bag. For example, if you want to attract wealth and money, use a green-colored string pouch. If you want to attract love, you can use a red one. The things you put into the mojo bag are entirely up to you. Here are some common elements that usually go into it.

- Oak leaves
- A stick of cinnamon
- Sunflower seeds and/or petals
- A horseshoe

You can add anything that you think will enhance the power and magic of your mojo bag. Put all the items into the drawstring pouch and dab or anoint it with your choice of essential oil, such as myrrh, cinnamon, benzoin, or prosperity oil.

"Parik-til translates to "holder of blessings." When you carry this bag, it means blessings follow you wherever you go. Therefore, hold the mojo bag you have created and feel the blessings emanating from it. Also, as you fill the drawstring bag with the items you have collected, you can chant a simple good luck mantra such as, *"I banish the bad clouds from my life, creating space for good luck. Come hither, come hither, good fortune, and fill my life with joy and happiness."*

Gypsy Spell to Make Your Dreams Come True

- Sit down for this ritual on a full moon day.
- Light a white candle, ensuring that all artificial lights are switched off.
- Write your wish on a piece of paper.
- For about ten minutes, watch the candle flame and visualize the fulfillment of your dream. Then say loudly, *"As I lay down in bed tonight, may the cosmic energies combine to make my dream come true."*
- Then, focus on your dream and burn the paper in the candle flame. Leave the candle to burn out completely.
- Repeat this ritual for twelve nights consecutively, starting from the full moon day.

Making amulets and talismans are all part of gypsy magic, and you can create your own depending on your need and the raw materials you have. You do not have to buy expensive stuff; t choose what appeals to your heart, use the right colors, candles, and essential oils, create a powerful intent, and transfer your personal power and dreams to the amulet/talisman you create. Wear it or carry it around so that the cosmic energies aligned with your intention find their way to you.

Chapter 6: Magical Herbs and Plants - A Little Herbal Grimoire

Gypsies have always relied on Mother Earth for their survival much more than normal settlers. Wherever they went, gypsies learned about and harnessed the power of common herbs and plants and used them in their magical and non-magical practices. Most gypsies have the skill and knowledge associated with using herbs and plants.

Gypsies learned about and harnessed the power of common herbs and plants.
https://www.pexels.com/photo/white-and-brown-ceramic-bowl-1793035/

If you want to learn the way of the Roma, mastering the knowledge of herbs and plants is vital. This chapter is dedicated to giving you a small grimoire of magical herbs and plants used by the Romani people.

Acacia — Acacia (also known as Arabic Gum) is used for spiritual and psychic enhancement and protection. It is great for rituals involving friendship, platonic love, and money. It's further used to aid in meditation.

Acorn — Acorn is a protective herb used in rituals related to personal power, wisdom, and good luck. Carry a dried acorn in your purse as an amulet to have youthful vigor and vim.

Alder — Alder trees are associated with divination and magic. They are also used in funeral rituals for the protection of spirits.

Ague — Ague is used in amulets for protection against evil and negative energies. It is used by itself or mixed with incense to break hexes and curses.

Almond — Almonds (also known as Shakad and Greek Nuts) are used to attract money, prosperity, and fruitfulness. It invokes the healing powers of gods and goddesses. It is also used for overcoming addictions and dependencies. You can carry an almond in your bag or use it as incense to attract the people you want in your life.

Amaranth — Amaranth is widely used in gypsy magic in various rituals, including healing broken hearts and summoning spirits.

Apple — Apples are used in rituals to honor deities. During Samhain ceremonies, apples are frequently used because they are considered to be the food of the dead. Apples are burned during this festival because they are believed to be the souls of the dead. Burning apples facilitate the rebirth of souls in spring. In the world of gypsy magic, apples are also known as Fruit of the Gods, Silver Branch, the Tree of Love, etc.

Balm of Gilead — This medicinal resin is mentioned in the Hebrew Bible and has deep connotations in Judaism and Christianity. It symbolizes love, protection, and healing and is used in rituals dealing with the loss of loved ones. Balm of Gilead is used in a love sachet to heal broken hearts and attract new love. It is also used to anoint candles. When it is burned, it attracts spirits.

Balsam Fir — This plant is great for building courage and strength. It brings about positive changes in your life, and if you are stuck with a puzzling question or problem, you can use balsam fir to find new perspectives and insights. Balsam fir is also used as incense by burning it on a plate of coal.

Bamboo — Bamboo is used for good fortune and protection against curses and hexes. Carve a wish or dream on a piece of bamboo, bury it, and watch this wish come true in your life. Another simple way to use bamboo is to carry a small piece on your person to attract good luck.

Barley — Barley is great for protection, healing, and love rituals. Simply scatter barley in your ritual space to keep out evil. Take a few barley grains and make a string with them. Tie this string around a little rock and throw it into a lake, pond, river, or stream while visualizing negativity leaving your body and mind and getting dissolved into nothingness in the water.

Basil — Basil is one of the most powerful herbs in gypsy magic and is used in spells and rituals involving love and wealth. The magic of basil also helps eliminate fears and evil and, therefore, is regularly used in exorcism rituals. If you know your path is filled with danger and need to move forward, carry some basil for divine help. You can carry a few basil leaves to attract wealth and prosperity or for success in a job interview.

Bay leaf — Bay leaf enhances your psychic powers. It is also used in good luck spells and rituals. As in the ritual using bamboo, carve your wish on a bay leaf. Hold it for a while as you visualize this wish coming true. Then burn the leaf, all the while imagining your wish coming true. Gypsies sleep with a bay leaf under their pillows to facilitate prophetic dreams. Carry a bay leaf in your pocket or purse for protection against black magic.

Beeswax — In the olden days, beeswax was the only raw material available for making candles. In gypsy magic practice, beeswax is used as a base for herbal healing salves.

Birch — The Romani people used birch for various magic rituals performed for protection, purification, to cure infertility, and exorcism. Plant a birch tree outside your home to keep it safe from evil and negativity.

Black cohosh — This plant attracts love, enhances potency (make a love sachet and carry it in your pocket for this), and increases courage. Carry it in a purple bag to protect against accidents and keep yourself safe from those who want to harm you. Add some to your amulet for courage and strength. Sprinkle it all over your house or room to keep out negativity and the effects of the evil eye. Burn it as a love incense.

Blessed thistle — Used to protect against negativity, blessed thistle is used by gypsies to break curses and hexes. Carrying this herb on your person will build your strength. It is also known to increase sexual potency in men.

Borage — The power of borage renders you with courage and sharpens your psychic powers. Put some borage flowers in your bathwater to lift your mood/spirit, increase courage, and protect your house from evil.

Buckthorn — This plant is used for good luck in court matters. Place buckthorn in your home to keep out evil and negative forces. Use the following simple ritual to make a wish or a dream come true with buckthorn:

- Make an infusion or powder of buckthorn.
- Hold it in your hand and face east.
- Turn in a clockwise direction standing in the same place until you return to your original position, facing east.
- As you make the circle, sprinkle the powder or infusion around yourself while visualizing your dream or wish.

Cactus — Cacti plants are great protective plants. They facilitate chastity and banish bad luck. Grow a few cacti plants in your garden to prevent unwanted energies from entering your home. Place cacti plants in all four directions of your home or garden for all-around protection.

Calendula flowers — These flowers are excellent for court and legal matters. Carry some in your pocket while going to court for the case to be decided in your favor. Putting some flowers under your bed will make your dreams come true. Another ability of these flowers is to render you the power to understand the communication of birds. Place some under your feet to understand bird talk.

Camphor — Camphor is associated with divination, psychic awareness, and dreams. Burn camphor to purify the surroundings. It also increases your power of persuasion. Add camphor to water when you are scrying.

Caraway — These seeds are great for rituals associated with love, passion, health, and memory. It has anti-theft properties as well. Place some caraway seeds in your safe or sprinkle some seeds around your house to keep out thieves. Caraway seeds are used in rituals and spells involving love and romance as they bring lovers closer to each other. Gypsies use caraway seeds to consecrate their magical tools and knickknacks. You can carry it in a small sachet to improve memory. Place the bag under your pillow to recall your dreams.

Carnation — This flower is for healing, strength, protection, and balance. Burn it as incense to enhance your creativity.

Catnip — This plant is sacred to Bast, the ancient Egyptian cat deity. Catnip is regularly used in all rituals dealing with cats or cat deities. Catnip and rose petals in love sachets both give amazing results. Combined with Dragon's Tree, it aids in eliminating bad habits and behavioral problems. Growing catnip in your garden or near your home's entrance is great for attracting good luck and the blessings of benevolent spirits.

Cedar — Cedar is for power, confidence, money, purification, and healing. Cedar is used for consecrating wands. Make sachets to promote peace and calm. Hanging a branch of cedar in your home will give protection against lightning.

Celandine — Celandine is an excellent herb to cure depression and for assistance in legal matters. It brings joy and victory. Carry celandine with you to build self-confidence, especially when meeting adversaries. Celandine is a great aid when you are doing ritual work to release yourself or someone else from feelings of being trapped. However, please note that celandine is a poison and, therefore, should be used very, very cautiously. If you have even a grain of doubt, do NOT use celandine anywhere unless you are under the supervision of a trained and qualified person.

Chamomile — Chamomile is used to reduce stress, to heal, and in love matters. Burning chamomile as incense attracts wealth. Use chamomile in spells related to success and to break hexes and curses. If you want your gambling efforts to bear fruit, chamomile can be useful. Before picking cards in a game of poker, remember to wash your hands with chamomile infusion.

Chicory — Chicory's magical powers are excellent for promoting positive perspectives and enhancing your sense of humor. Anoint yourself with an infusion of chicory if you want to receive favors from others.

Cinnamon — Cinnamon is a spice that works excellently in rituals and spellwork involving healing, spirituality, love, power, luck, protection, passion, and wisdom. Burn cinnamon during meditation sessions to raise spiritual awareness, enhance your psychic powers, and attract money.

Cloves — Cloves are used in banishing rituals, achieving dreams, and protection. Burn cloves to eliminate gossip and its harmful effects on your life. It also cleanses the aura and enhances the spiritual vibrations of the area. String a few cloves together and hang them over baby cribs for protection. Carry it to attract love and help you during bereavement.

Daffodils — Daffodils stand for fertility, love, and good luck. Wear the flower near your heart to attract love into your life. Place fresh daffodils in any home where the inhabitants are trying to get pregnant. The flowers increase fertility.

Dandelion leaf — Bury some dandelion leaves in your garden or any other suitable place to keep your home safe from evil forces and negativity. They are great in spells involving making your wishes and dreams come true.

Dill — Dill is the herb for money, passion or lust, and protection. It is commonly used in house blessing rituals as it keeps out negativity. Dill also helps to discern mindless superstition and real magic. Dill seeds can be used in money spells to attract wealth. If you want a night of passion, smell dill seeds before bed. You can also add some dill seeds to your bath. Bathe in this water before a date, and you will be irresistible to your date.

Dragon's blood — Dragon's blood is burned as incense to enhance the potency of any spell or ritual because of its strong banishing power to eliminate negativity and evil. It is used in rituals dealing with eliminating bad habits and bad influences.

Elder — Elder is used in house and business blessing ceremonies. It is good for releasing enchantments and protection against negativity. It also helps the wearer deal with temptations to commit adultery. It's also used in funeral rites to help the departed soul's journey to the other world. A word of extreme caution about this: Elder roots, bark, and raw berries are poisonous, so they must be used with utmost care. If you are unsure, do not use it.

Elm — Elm is used by gypsy magic practitioners to connect with the world of the elves. If you want to stop someone from spreading bad rumors about you, you can use this simple spell: Write the person's name on an elm leaf and bury it in a safe place. The slander will stop. Elm is also used for protection against lightning and to attract love.

Eucalyptus — Eucalyptus attracts healing vibrations. To do this, sprinkle some dried eucalyptus around a lit blue candle. Eucalyptus oil is a great purifier, too. Eucalyptus leaves are a great addition to dream pillows and healing bags/sachets. Put a few leaves into your amulet to heal and reconcile differences in relationships.

Fenugreek — Fenugreek is used for rituals and spells to attract money and improve fertility. Put some fenugreek seeds around your home to attract wealth. Find a small jar and fill it with some fenugreek seeds. Add some fenugreek seeds every day into this jar. Money will never stop flowing into your home.

Feverfew — Feverfew is used for protection against colds, fevers, flu, and accidents. Keep some of these flowers in your luggage and car while traveling.

Flaxseed — Flaxseed is used in healing and money rituals. Flaxseeds keep out poverty from the home. Place a small bottle of flaxseeds for this purpose. Flaxseed enhances the accuracy of divination rituals and outcomes. Sprinkle an infusion of flaxseed in and around a divination ritual space before the start of the ritual.

Garlic — The magical power of garlic has long since been reputed to repulse vampires and is also used in exorcism rituals. It guards against negative and hostile magic. Hang some garlic pods in your home to keep the family united. When you wear garlic while traveling out, it keeps bad weather at bay. Gypsies used fresh garlic to heal the sick by rubbing fresh garlic over the sick person's body. The garlic absorbs the sickness from the individual, which can then be discarded safely.

Ginseng — Ginseng's magical uses include beauty, love, and healing. Carry some ginseng to attract love and increase libido. Carve your wish into ginseng root and throw it in water. Your wish will come true.

Holly — Plant holly in your home or garden for protective purposes. It is also used in love, marriage, and good luck magic. Males with low sexual libido are asked to carry holly plants in their pockets, which is believed to enhance their sexual prowess.

Hyacinth — Hyacinth, named after the Greek god of same-sex love and intimacy, is the flower for love and good luck. Hyacinth is the patron herb of homosexuals. Wear hyacinth flowers to protect yourself against nightmares. Its magical powers are also used to help with labor pains.

Hyssop — Hyssop is the most commonly used purification herb in gypsy magic. It promotes spiritual opening and enhances the power of vibrations. Therefore, it is the most sought-after herb to consecrate magical tools and items. Just sprinkling an infusion of hyssop on objects and people is great to cleanse and purify them. Hang some hyssop in your home to protect it from burglars and trespassers.

Irish moss — Irish moss is an amazing good luck herb. Place some Irish moss under your rug to attract wealth into your home. Carry some for protection when you travel. Irish moss is used to stuff sachets or poppets made for money or love. Sprinkle an infusion of Irish moss around your business place to get increased footfalls.

Jasmine — Jasmine is used in rituals involving snakebite antidotes and for divination work. Jasmine is commonly used to charge quartz crystals. Use jasmine flowers in sachets to attract your soulmate. Burning dried jasmine leaves before sleeping helps to induce prophetic dreams. It also improves creativity and promotes innovation.

Kava Kava — Kava Kava can form a potent sacramental drink and is made as a magical potion that can induce astral work and visions. Carry it with you when traveling for protection, promotions, and career success.

Lavender — The magical uses of lavender are in the realms of love, protection, peace, and healing. Lavender is known to alleviate symptoms of depression. Sprinkle some lavender oil in your bath and have a restful sleep. When combined with rosemary, it prevents lovers from straying. If you are anxious or worried, burn lavender flowers as incense to feel calm and peaceful. The ashes of the burned flowers can be sprinkled around your home to attract harmony and tranquility.

Lotus — Lotus is sacred to many cultures, including Egyptian, Indian, etc. Lotus flowers adorn many Indian and Egyptian gods. It is very useful for spiritual and psychic growth, love, and protection.

Myrrh — Myrrh is used for spiritual awakening or opening, healing, and meditation. Thanks to high vibrations of psychic powers, myrrh works well to enhance the power and energy of all magic rituals and workings. Myrrh smoke can be used to cleanse and bless talismans and amulets. Usually, myrrh and frankincense are burned together as incense.

Marigold — This flower attracts admiration and respect and works well in court and legal matters. Add an infusion of marigolds into your bathwater to attract love. This flower is excellent to use in love sachets and amulets to attract new love and intensify love and romance in an existing relationship.

Mugwort — Mugwort can be carried around to cure insanity and other mental illnesses. It is also good for lust and fertility. Placing mugwort near divination and scrying tools will enhance their powers. Rubbing an infusion of mugwort on objects is excellent for ridding negativity and cleansing the magical aura of crystal balls and magic mirrors.

Oak — Oak is believed to be the most sacred of all trees. Oak wood is used to build many magical tools. Burn oak leaves to purify the surroundings. This will help to strengthen family unity. It also reduces sibling and family rivalry. Carry some oak in your pocket to keep yourself young and healthy. It helps to gain strength and wisdom.

Passion Flower — As the name suggests, this flower is great for increasing libido and attracting friendship and prosperity. Place some passion flowers in your house to bring calm and reduce conflicts and arguments. You can use an infusion of passion flowers as a wash to reduce stress and arguments. Place some passion flowers under your pillow for better sleep. Add some infusion into your bath for five days to attract lovers.

Peppermint — Place peppermint in pillows to aid restful sleep and for prophetic dreams. Peppermint oil can be used to anoint household objects and home furnishings. It is burned as incense to enhance the vibrations of sacred spaces and for healing and protection.

Rosemary — Rosemary is worn to improve memory and, therefore, is excellent for students. It is also used to create dream pillows to prevent nightmares and is good for spells and rituals connected to health, love, and passion. Rosemary is burned as incense before rituals for purification and cleansing purposes. Before any ritual, for added protection, you should wash your hands with an infusion of rosemary.

Saffron — Saffron is a great aphrodisiac and is useful for dealing with love, happiness, strength, and healing. You can carry a small amount of saffron for increased psychic awareness. If you are sad or depressed, washing your hands with saffron-infused water will attract happiness.

Sage — Sage is one of the most common herbs used for purifying. It can also help in dealing with grief and loss. Sage promotes spiritual, mental, and physical health. Write your wish on a sage leaf and place it under your pillow. Do this for three nights for your dreams and wishes to come true. However, if you do not dream about your wish, remember to bury the sage to prevent any harm. Carry some sage for wisdom and improved clarity. Sage is used as an incense to clear and cleanse ritual spaces before the start of magic work.

Sandalwood — The Romani people sprinkle sandalwood powder around their wagons to keep out negativity. You can use a piece of sandalwood to heal broken wands. It facilitates concentration and, therefore, is good for meditation. Your wish can come true if you try the following wishing spell with sandalwood: Take a small piece of sandalwood and carve your wish on it. Then burn it, and visualize your wish coming true as it burns.

Tea leaves — Tea leaves used in amulets and talismans are great for building courage and strength. It is also known to increase libido, making it perfect for making drinks related to lust and passion. Burning tea leaves attracts wealth and money.

Vervain — Vervain is used for sleep, wealth and money, youth-related stuff, peace, purification, and protection. Keep some in your home for protection against storms and lightning. If you are having nightmares, place some vervain under your pillow. Put some vervain in your bathwater for mental and emotional cleansing, especially before practicing magic. You can put some in amulets for protection, especially for children.

Willow — The willow is believed to be a sacred wishing tree and is perfect for moon magic and divination work. It helps to attract and strengthen love and overcome sadness, grief, and depression. Wear a sprig of willow when you have to deal with the death or loss of a loved one.

Yucca — This plant is used in rituals and spell work involving purification, protection, and transmutation. Use yucca fibers to make a crucifix and hang it on your main door for protection against evil and negativity. Before doing a magical ritual, cleanse and purify your body with an infusion of yucca.

Finally, here is a very important word of caution. Do not consume any of the herbs, plants, and plant parts mentioned in this chapter without seeking medical advice. Burning incense also requires maximum supervision, caution, and care. Therefore, avoid it, especially in the beginner stage.

Chapter 7: Gypsy Tarot I. The Cards

Now that you have a good idea of the basics of gypsy magic, let us dive into the gypsy divinatory practices, starting with tarot. Reading tarot cards conjures images of old, shriveled, white-haired women wearing headscarves and looking into crystal balls. Yes, gypsy witches might have dressed like this, and, of course, there is an aura of mysticism around tarot cards. Yet, tarot readings give an insight into the various forces in your current state of life and guide you to make sensible, informed choices for yourself and your loved ones.

Tarot readings are great to give an insight into the various forces in play in your current state of life.
https://www.pexels.com/photo/assorted-tarot-cards-on-table-3088369/

Different Types of Tarot Card Decks

Over the years, multiple decks have been developed by different cultures around the world. Let us look at some of them in this section.

Rider-Waite Deck — The most popular deck available is the Rider-Waite Deck. It comprises the classic Major and Minor Arcana. It was first published by Arthur Edward Waite, a mystic and academic. The illustrations were done by Pamela Coleman Smith, and her name is now synonymous with tarot cards.

Thoth Tarot — This tarot deck was designed and outlined by the English magician and occultist Aleister Crowley and was first published in 1969. The illustrations were done by Lady Freida Harris, who created, modified, and recreated drawings according to Crowley's specifications.

The Wild Unknown — This deck is inspired and drawn from the ancient animal spirit and animal wisdom to interpret the present and portend future possibilities. It was illustrated and created by Kim Krans and first published in 2012.

The Enchanted Tarot — The Enchanted Tarot was created by the husband-wife team of Amy Zerner and Monte Farber. The cards were designed on the premise that whatever question a seeker has at a particular moment, the cards will reveal the answers and situations connected to that question. Tarot readings through this deck need not be done in person: Online readings are also possible because the intention is what matters.

The New Mythic Tarot — Illustrated by the internationally acclaimed Greek artist Giovanni Caselli, the New Mythic Tarot card deck features gods, goddesses, heroes, and demigods from Greek mythology.

As mentioned earlier, the first deck, the Rider-Waite deck, is the most popular, and most tarot readers use this.

Structure of the Deck

Here, let us briefly explore the structure of the deck, which is primarily categorized into the Major Arcana and the Minor Arcana.

The Major Arcana

The Major Arcana is the most easily recognizable set of cards in the tarot deck. The mystical messages they carry and express are both impactful and powerful. The twenty-two cards of the Major Arcana reflect different aspects of human life. The pictures and messages of the Major

Arcana cards give you an amazing insight into your life path, dreams, purposes, obstacles preventing you from your purposes, destiny, and more.

Although each of the twenty-two cards in this subset of the tarot deck carries a specific message that guides you in your journey of life, collectively, they also tell you a story. The Fool, the first of the twenty-two cards, is the protagonist of this story. The Major Arcana is a journey of the Fool as he meets with each card.

As he moves through the remaining twenty-one cards, he grows and learns from life experiences. The story describes the various setbacks and accomplishments we face in our lifetime, all of which contribute to completing our fully-rounded personalities. Following is a brief description of the twenty-two Major Arcana cards:

Card #0 – The Fool – The first card in the Major Arcana, the Fool represents the most vulnerable aspects of ourselves. The Fool is inexperienced and unaware of his strengths, weaknesses, and potential. When you draw the Fool card, it usually calls for openness and willingness to embrace everything that will happen in the future and learn the lessons that the events and experiences are trying to teach you.

Card #1 – The Magician – The second Major Arcana card reminds you that you are unique and special. It tells you that you have it in you to do what it takes and get what you want. Your gifts and talents set you apart from the crowd. The Magician card tells you not to waste these skills and that you must harness them to begin new projects and/or overcome challenges and adversity. When you draw the Magician card, you should not wait any longer: You should move forward and accomplish your goals.

Card #2 – The High Priestess – This indicates our subconscious mind and awareness. It is the most intuitive card in the entire tarot card deck. It reminds you that your mind knows far more than you think. This card indicates that you should follow your heart and trust your instincts. If you draw the High Priestess card, it's a sign to stop looking outward and turn inward to find the answers you seek.

Card #3 – The Empress – The Empress, deeply connected to Mother Earth, manifests all things feminine, including beauty, love, and compassion. The Empress urges you to embrace everything the world offers you in any given situation so that you can harness all the energy to achieve your desired outcomes.

Card #4 — The Emperor — The Emperor stands for authority and power. This card is a sign of organizational power and leadership. This card reminds you that just like an emperor, you must also face and overcome challenges to become the king of your life. If you get this card, it is a message that you also hold great control over your life and how you want it to pan out.

Card #5 — The Hierophant — The Hierophant is a messenger from the heavens who carries the wisdom, spirituality, and knowledge he gained there to the human world. If you draw the Hierophant card, it indicates following the rules and regulations in that particular situation if you have to win. Moreover, it's also an indication to find a spiritual perspective of the circumstance under consideration.

Card #6 — The Lovers — The Lovers card does not just represent romantic relationships but all of life's close relationships. If you get this card, it means you need to focus on your love life. Normally, the Lovers card is drawn when you are at some crossroads in your life and is a reminder to recall your life's values and principles. The Lovers card urges you not to make hasty decisions and wrong choices. It tells you that it's your duty to look at all possible angles of a given problem and make informed, sensible choices.

Card #7 — The Chariot — Like a fast-moving chariot, this card is the manifestation of human determination and drive. If you pick the Chariot card, it could indicate an upcoming successful event or victorious endeavor. This card also reminds you that your greatest successes do not come from limited or narrow thinking. It tells you that if you combine the power of your mind, spirit, and heart, nothing can stop you.

Card #8 — Strength — As the name suggests, this card represents strength, though not necessarily physical strength. It is indicative of the power and strength of your heart and how courageous you are. It indicates your willpower and ability to deal with whatever life throws at you. If you pick this card during a tarot reading, it's a message that you have the strength to deal with whatever you are facing right now and will come out stronger and more powerful.

Card #9 — The Hermit — The Hermit loves solitude because he knows it is possible to find solutions and answers in deep silence. The Hermit card tells you that the best way to understand and process everything happening in your life is to withdraw from the chaos and noise. It tells you to find your place of solitude so that you can turn inward and discover the answers to your questions and solutions to your worries.

Card #10 — Wheel of Fortune — The Wheel of Fortune reminds you that life and circumstances are always changing like a rotating wheel. Sometimes, you find yourself at the top, and sometimes, at the bottom. This card tells you that nothing is permanent, and everything, good and bad, comes to an end. It is important to learn all the lessons that life experiences are trying to teach you.

Card #11 — Justice — The Justice card is a reminder that what goes around comes around. It tells you that every action and non-action has consequences. Your present life and what you are experiencing are the result of your past decisions and actions, and they are exactly what you deserve. If you draw this card, it is an indication that you need to examine everything in your life and ensure that you are as fair as you can be.

Card #12 — The Hanged Man — This card usually comes up when you are in limbo and unsure what to do in any given situation. If you draw this card, you are uncertain what to do or where to begin. In such cases, always begin with letting go. Letting go can be in the form of loosening your grip over something or letting go of the results and consequences of your actions. The Hanged Man reminds you that small sacrifices have to be made for the bigger picture to emerge in your favor.

Card #13 — Death — Sadly, this is one of the most misunderstood cards in the tarot deck. The Death card does not stand for physical death. It symbolizes cycles that have both beginnings and endings. While death does stand for endings, you must remind yourself that endings also mean the start of something new. Therefore, when you get the Death Card, it could mean that it is time to give up holding on to old relationships that do not serve your purpose anymore. It means it's time to let old, bitter, and unpleasant feelings and memories die so that your heart and mind are ready to accept new, beautiful things.

Card #14 — Temperance — As the name suggests, this card stands for patience and peace. If you draw this card, it is an indication for you to go with the flow, not to resist things and events happening in your life, and not to force anything to happen. The Temperance card is a clear sign that you must take things as they come to you, be flexible, and adapt sensibly to the changes in your life.

Card #15 — The Devil — If you draw this card, it could indicate that you feel powerless and constrained. If you pick this card, you will likely feel powerless and trapped in a situation you do not want to be in. The

Devil is trying to convince you that you have no options. However, that is a lie. It is your life, and you can take back control of it. The feelings of being trapped have nothing to do with external forces. They come only with your internal limitations and the unwillingness to change, move forward, or see another perspective. The keys to unlocking your life are in your hands. You hold your freedom.

Card #16 — The Tower — The Tower represents destruction and is the most dreaded card in the tarot deck. It is normally drawn when all aspects of your life seem to be crumbling down, and there is nothing you can do about it. This card tells you to let things fall because the destruction also allows you to kill your weaknesses. Sometimes, you have to be an iconoclast to challenge and break down things completely so that you can use the remnants to build a better and stronger thing.

Card #17 — The Star — This card, representing healing and hope, calms and soothes. It brings renewal, optimism, and inspiration. This card means you are on the right side of the universe and that the cosmos is working for you. It is aligned with your needs and desires. Follow where your life is leading you.

Card #18 — The Moon — This card represents your subconscious mind and manifests your suppressed fears, doubts, feelings, and thoughts. If you pick the Moon card, it could mean that you are allowing your fears and doubts to overwhelm you and make you anxious. These fears might override your past happy memories and faith in a happy future. Draw these internalized feelings and thoughts to the surface, address them maturely and wisely, and worries and anxieties will disappear.

Card #19 — The Sun — This card of light and love represents optimism and happiness. If you pick this card, it means you are in a happy place in your life, and things are working in your favor. It means you are moving in the right direction. Listen to this uplifting card and identify and be grateful for the good things and people in your life.

Card #20 — Judgment — This card represents your past and future coming together. If you get this card, it is time to review what has been happening in your life, including your choices and actions, and see if everything is aligned with your ultimate life purpose and where you want to go. This card is a reminder that nothing is cast in stone, and you can change for the better at any time in your life.

Card #21 — The World — This card is a manifestation of a full circle of completing something fully and taking the fruits of your labor. This card means that you are exactly where you are supposed to be. It means that your self-awareness is high, and you have a much better understanding of yourself and the world around you than before. It means you are ready for the next phase of your life.

The Minor Arcana

The "minor" in Minor Arcana does not in any way take away the importance of these cards. In fact, of the 78 cards in a tarot deck, the majority belong to the Minor Arcana. The cards of the Minor Arcana provide you with insights into your life experiences in the short term. For example, it is useful to see how your day or week is going to be. It indicates what kind of struggles, obstacles, and successes you will likely face in the upcoming few days.

When you start with a tarot card reading every morning, the Minor Arcana card you draw will help you give your best to that particular day, no matter what bad and/or good experiences await you. The Minor Arcana in a tarot card deck is divided into four sets of fourteen cards each. The sets called "Suits" in the language of tarot cards comprise the Suit of Pentacles, the Suit of Swords, the Suit of Cups, and the Suit of Wands. Each of the four Suits is made up of the following:

- Numbered cards from one to ten. Number one is referred to as the Ace.
- Four court cards, including the King, Queen, Knight, and Page.

The Suit of Wands — The cards in this suit give you an indication of when to take action and when to lie low and hold back. It is the suit that deals with action and initiative.

The Cups — The Suit of Cups indicates elements concerning emotions, relationships, and intuition. The cards in the Suit of Cups give you the right direction in love matters and help you deal with all your emotions, from the smallest to the biggest.

The Swords — The Suit of Swords symbolizes challenges. They give you an indication of impending challenges and obstacles you are likely to face and how to harness your powers to overcome them.

The Pentacles — The Suit of Pentacles deals with finances, profession, and career. These cards answer questions related to your family, wealth, health, and long-term material goals.

So, each of these suits is an indicator of certain aspects of your life. The numbered and court cards show you exactly what energy patterns are affecting the aspects of your life. Let us look at the fourteen cards and see what they mean.

Aces (1) — Ones or aces usually mean the current period of the seeker (whether you or someone else) is at the start of a new adventure or venture. The card of Aces also indicates drive and determination.

Twos (2) — The card of Twos has two conflicting connotations. It means a dichotomous situation and also stands for balance. Therefore, you cannot move forward until the balance is achieved.

Threes (3) — Threes stand for interactions and communication and how your interactions with others affect all aspects of your life, including social, professional, and personal.

Fours (4) — A card of Fours stands for a break or rest. Rest and contemplation are essential for any journey to be successful. When you get a four card, it is time to take a step back and reconnoiter.

Fives (5) — Drawing a card of Fives means a time of conflict and adversity. This card tells you that it is time to draw up all of your energy reserves to deal with negative and unpleasant experiences. It could mean an upcoming loss, too.

Sixes (6) — Sixes stand for growth and development. It also means that you must find your inner resolve to beat the current obstacles and challenges to grow and develop.

Sevens (7) — This card is an indicator of your self-confidence. It tells you that regardless of the unpleasant things and events taking place in your life, you have the wherewithal to overcome everything, move forward, and achieve your dreams.

Eights (8) — This card tells you to prepare for changes. It tells you that change is constant, and only when you change and adapt will you find success and happiness. This card could be an indication that you need to reassess your current situation and change how you deal with it.

Nines (9) — This card is an indicator of all things, and your efforts are set to come together toward some sort of outcome(s). Of course, the result may not be something you expect or like.

Tens (10) — This card represents a finish line or the end of a cycle or period. It means you will receive the fruits and consequences of your efforts and actions.

Pages — When you get a Page card, you know what you want but are unsure how to get it. The Page card is a message that you must gather all the information and resources you need and then take the necessary steps to achieve your goals.

Knights — When you draw the Knights card, it is time to start work, take action, and set the wheels in motion. The Knight stands for movement, and you have to set about moving to get to where you want to go.

Queens — The Queen card represents your inner potential. However, it also means that you cannot do things alone. It tells you that it is time to seek the counsel of the wise and experienced people in your life.

Kings — This is a card of authority and power. It reminds you of your inner power and tells you to harness it to achieve your goals and desires.

Reading tarot cards involves many layers of understanding, including what you want to see and hear. Your instincts play a big part, too. The information in this chapter is a simple presentation of the various "tools" of interpretations.

It is entirely up to you, the reader, to come up with your own interpretations by tapping into your intuition and associating the meaning of the suite with the meaning of the card's number. The next chapter will delve deeper into this aspect.

Chapter 8: Gypsy Tarot II - Reading the Cards

In this chapter, you will learn how to read the cards like a gypsy. The Major and Minor Arcana cards hold life meanings and answers to our questions. When they are drawn and read together, they give credible messages that point in the direction of the answers we seek when consulting tarot cards. The ability to interpret the meanings of the cards drawn lies within each of our internal belief systems and narratives. So, let us get started.

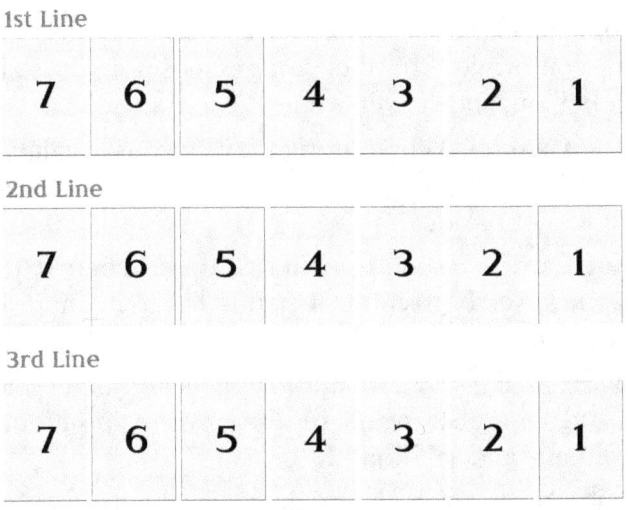

Start by looking at each of the cards and understanding what they mean. Focus on the illustration in detail. Next, focus on each card and think of its meaning both facing up and when reversed. Let's look at the 78 cards for this purpose.

Interpreting the Major Arcana

The Fool Card — When upright, it stands for innocence, a free spirit, and new beginnings. An upright Fool Card means you must get ready for a new adventure. When reversed, it stands for inconsideration, recklessness, and being taken advantage of or for granted.

The Magician Card — When upright, it symbolizes creation, desire, willpower, and manifestation. A reversed Magician Card stands for being out of touch, trickery, and illusion.

The High Priestess Card — When upright, it represents your inner voice, the subconscious mind, and your intuition. In the reverse position, the High Priestess Card represents repressed feelings, not being centered, and the disconnection from your inner voice.

The Empress Card — When upright, it symbolizes Mother Nature, fertility, and motherhood. In the reverse position, this card stands for a nosy attitude, smothering, dependence, and emptiness.

The Emperor Card — When upright, it represents fatherhood, structure, authority, and control. In the reverse position, it stands for coldness, tyranny, and rigidity.

The Hierophant Card — When upright, it stands for ethics, morals, tradition, and conformity. In the reverse position, it stands for new approaches, rebellion, and subversiveness.

The Lovers Card — When upright, it means duality, union, and partnerships. In the reverse position, it symbolizes disharmony, one-sidedness, and loss of balance.

The Chariot Card — When upright, it implies control, direction, and willpower. In the reverse position, it stands for aggression and a lack of control or direction.

The Strength Card — When upright, it is all about focus, bravery, compassion, and inner strength. In the reverse position, it is about insecurity, weakness, and self-doubt.

The Hermit Card — When upright, it is about inner guidance, the search for truth, and contemplation. In the reverse position, it is about losing your way, loneliness, and isolation.

The Wheel of Fortune Card — When upright, it stands for the inevitability of destiny, cycles, and changes. In the reverse position, it implies bad luck, clinging on to control, and losing control.

The Justice Card — When upright, it represents truth, clarity, and cause and effect (or consequences). In the reverse position, it stands for unfairness, dishonesty, and unaccountability.

The Hanged Man Card — When upright, it stands for martyrdom, sacrifice, and release. In the reverse position, it can be interpreted as fear, a needless sacrifice, or stalling.

The Death Card — When upright, it represents metamorphosis, change, the end of cycles, and new beginnings. In the reverse position, it stands for decay, stagnation, holding on, and fear of change.

The Temperance Card — When upright, it stands for the search to find true meaning, patience, and the middle, balanced path. In the reverse position, it stands for lack of balance, extremes, and excesses.

The Devil Card — When upright, it represents playfulness, materialism, and addiction. In the reverse position, it manifests restoring control, release, and freedom.

The Tower Card — When upright, it represents disaster, sudden upheaval, and broken pride. In the reverse position, it manifests fear of suffering, delayed disaster, or avoided disaster.

The Star Card — When upright, it stands for rejuvenation, hope, and faith. In the reverse position, it represents insecurity, faithlessness, and discouragement.

The Moon Card — When upright, it manifests intuition, illusions, and the unconscious mind. In the reverse position, it stands for misinterpretation, confusion, and fear.

The Sun Card — When upright, it means positivity, joy, success, and celebration. In the reverse position, it stands for sadness, depression, and negativity.

The Judgment Card — When upright, it stands for awakening, reckoning, and reflection. In the reverse position, it stands for self-loathing, low self-awareness, and self-doubt.

The World Card — When upright, it stands for completion, harmony, and fulfillment. In the reverse position, it symbolizes the lack of closure and restlessness about things not being completed.

Interpreting the Minor Arcana

The Suit of Wands

The wand symbolizes our innate power to draw the primal, cosmic energy that gets redirected in the form of passion, willpower, and inspiration inside us, all of which play an important role in leading happy, meaningful, purpose-filled lives. The Suit of Wands is representative of the fire element. Fire also stands for action and purpose. Therefore, the cards in this suit indicate your ambitions and subsequent plans of action.

Ace of Wands — When upright, it represents desire, inspiration, willpower, and creation. Reversed, it could mean boredom and a lack of energy and passion.

Two of Wands — When upright, it stands for leaving home, making decisions, and planning. Reversed, it means bad planning, fear of change, or playing safe.

Three of Wands — When upright, it represents rapid growth, looking ahead, and expansion. Reversed, it means frustration, obstacles, and delays.

Four of Wands — When upright, it represents celebration, community, and home. Reversed, it stands for conflicts at home, lack of support, and transience.

Five of Wands — When upright, it stands for rivalry, competition, and conflict. Reversed, it manifests respecting differences, conflict, and avoidance.

Six of Wands — When upright, it represents public reward, success, and victory. Reversed, it stands for punishment, lack of recognition, and excess pride.

Seven of Wands — When upright, it manifests control, defensiveness, and perseverance. Reversed, it manifests being overwhelmed, giving up, and destruction.

Eight of Wands — When upright, it means that you need to make some fast decisions or quick actions. Reversed, it stands for slowing down, waiting, and panicking.

Nine of Wands — When upright, it stands for grit and resilience. Reversed, it manifests doubtful motivations, fatigue, and exhaustion.

Ten of Wands — When upright, it stands for burden, responsibility, and accomplishment. Reversed, it stands for burnout, being overstressed, and the inability to delegate.

Page of Wands — When upright, it can be interpreted as freedom, excitement, and exploration. Reversed, it means conflict, lack of direction, and procrastination.

Knight of Wands — When upright, it stands for fearlessness, action, and adventure. Reversed, it manifests recklessness, impulsiveness, and anger.

Queen of Wands — When upright, it stands for joy, determination, and courage. Reversed, it means insecurities, jealousies, and selfishness.

King of Wands — When upright, it stands for overcoming challenges, leadership, and seeing the big picture. Reversed, it manifests unachievable goals and expectations, impulsiveness, and an overbearing attitude.

The Suit of Cups

The Suit of Cups is connected with creativity, intuition, and emotions and represents the water element. Cards from this suit speak about romantic, family, and platonic relationships and imagination. In a worst-case scenario, the Suit of Cups cards deal with uncontrollable feelings.

Ace of Cups — When upright, it means intuition, spirituality, and new beginnings. Reversed, it means emptiness, blockages in creativity, and emotional loss.

Two of Cups — When upright, it represents connection, unity, and partnerships. Reversed, it stands for tension, imbalance, and broken communication.

Three of Cups — When upright, it stands for happiness, community, and friendship. Reversed, it manifests isolation, gossip, and overindulgence.

Four of Cups — When upright, it stands for disconnectedness, apathy, and contemplation. Reversed, it stands for acceptance, sudden revelation or awareness, and choosing happiness.

Five of Cups — When upright, it can be interpreted as self-pity, grief, or loss. Reversed, it stands for finding peace, moving on, and acceptance.

Six of Cups — When upright, it stands for healing, happy memories, and familiarity. Reversed, it stands for independence, leaving home, and moving forward.

Seven of Cups — When upright, it means daydreaming, having to make choices, and searching for purpose. Reversed, it means confusion, diversion from your path, and lack of purpose.

Eight of Cups — When upright, it means leaving behind, walking away, and disillusionment. Reversed, it means fear of loss, avoidance, and fear of change.

Nine of Cups — When upright, it means luxury, emotional stability, and satisfaction. Reversed, it means dissatisfaction, smugness, and lack of inner joy.

Ten of Cups — When upright, it stands for dreams coming true, inner happiness, and fulfillment. Reversed, it means domestic disharmony, broken family, and shattered dreams.

Page of Cups — When upright, it means sensitivity, dreaming, and an upcoming happy surprise. Reversed, it means disappointment, insecurity, and emotional immaturity.

Knight of Cups — When upright, it means romance, idealism, and following the heart. Reversed, it means disappointment and moodiness.

Queen of Cups — When upright, it means comfort, calm, and compassion. Reversed, it means dependence, insecurity, and martyrdom.

King of Cups — When upright, it means to control, balance, and compassion. Reversed, it means bad advice, coldness, and moodiness.

The Suit of Swords

Associated with the air element, the Suit of Swords deals with intelligence, truth, logic, ambition, communication, and conflict. Interestingly, this suit is called "sword," and intellect and logic are elements that can be used for evil or good purposes, like double-edged swords. In a worst-case scenario, cards from the Suit of Swords can mean a lack of empathy, harshness, and abuse.

Ace of Swords — When upright, it stands for a sharp mind, clarity, and breakthrough. Reversed, it stands for chaos, brutality, and confusion.

Two of Swords — When upright, it stands for stalemate, indecision, and difficult choices. Reversed, it means confusion, having to choose the lesser of two evils, and having no choice.

Three of Swords — When upright, it stands for grief, suffering, and heartbreak. Reversed, it stands for moving on, forgiveness, and recovery.

Four of Swords — When upright, it means a time of contemplation, rest, and restoration. Reversed, it means stress, burnout, and restlessness.

Five of Swords — When upright, it stands for sneakiness, wanting to win at all costs, and unbridled ambition. Reversed, it stands for the desire to forgive and reconcile and lingering resentment.

Six of Swords — When upright, it stands for moving on, leaving something behind, and transitioning. Reversed, it stands for resisting transition, unresolved issues, and emotional baggage.

Seven of Swords — When upright, it stands for trickery, strategy, tactics, and deception. Reversed, it stands for rethinking an approach and coming clean.

Eight of Swords — When upright, it means self-victimization, imprisonment, and entrapment. Reversed, it stands for freedom, new perspective, and self-acceptance.

Nine of Swords — When upright, it stands for trauma, anxiety, and hopelessness. Reversed, it stands for hope and reaching out.

Ten of Swords — When upright, it stands for defeat, collapse, and failure. Reversed, it means the inevitable end, the worst part is done and dusted, and only upward movement now.

Page of Swords — When upright, it stands for mental energy, restlessness, and curiosity. Reversed, it means all talk and no action, manipulation, and deception.

Knight of Swords — When upright, it means defending your beliefs, action, and impulsiveness. Reversed, it means unpredictability, no regard for consequences, and lack of direction.

Queen of Swords — When upright, it stands for clear-mindedness, perceptiveness, and complex situations. Reversed, it means bitterness, cruelty, and cold-heartedness.

King of Swords — When upright, it means truth, discipline, and putting the head over the heart in all matters. Reversed, it means weakness, cruelty, and manipulation.

The Suit of Pentacles

Associated with the earth element, the Suit of Pentacles deals with all materialistic and worldly things, including finances and money, stability, security, health, nature, and prosperity. The cards from this suit also usually indicate matters relating to your household and career. A reversed card indicates greed, unbridled ambition, miserliness, and jealousy.

Ace of Pentacles — When upright, it represents new ventures, prosperity, and opportunity. Reversed, it stands for a bad investment and missed/lost opportunity.

Two of Pentacles — When upright, it stands for adapting to change, priorities, and balancing decisions. Reversed, it manifests being overwhelmed, losing balance, and being disorganized.

Three of Pentacles — When upright, it represents collaboration and teamwork. Reversed, it manifests group or team conflict, disorganization, and lack of teamwork.

Four of Pentacles — When upright, it means security, frugality, and conservation. Reversed, it stands for possessiveness, miserliness, and greed.

Five of Pentacles — When upright, it stands for insecurity, poverty, and need. Reversed, it means improvement, charity, and recovery.

Six of Pentacles — When upright, it manifests sharing, generosity, and charity. Reversed, it stands for domination and power, miserliness, and strings attached to help or support.

Seven of Pentacles — When upright, it stands for diligence, perseverance, and hard work. Reversed, it stands for not getting rewards or working without results and with distractions.

Eight of Pentacles — When upright, it means high standards, passion, and apprenticeship. Reversed, it means a lack of motivation, passion, or feeling or being uninspired.

Nine of Pentacles — When upright, it represents luxury, rewards, and fruits of labor. Reversed, it means false success, living beyond one's means, and excessive spending.

Ten of Pentacles — When upright, it means inheritance, legacy, and culmination. Reversed, it stands for lack of resources, instability, and fleeting success.

Page of Pentacles — When upright, it manifests diligence, desire, and ambition. Reversed, it stands for laziness, greed, and lack of commitment.

Knight of Pentacles — When upright, it stands for responsibility, hard work, and efficiency. Reversed, it stands for work without rewards, obsessiveness, and laziness.

Queen of Pentacles — When upright, it means financial comfort, creature comforts, and practicality. Reversed, it means smothering, self-centeredness, and jealousy.

King of Pentacles — When upright, it means security, prosperity, and abundance. Reversed, it means sensuality, greed, and indulgence.

Keep reading and learning about the messages and interpretations of each of the 78 cards in your tarot deck. The more you read, the more you will connect with the cards you draw, and the better your interpretations will be.

Shuffling the Deck

Before any reading, it is imperative that you shuffle the tarot card deck. This seemingly simple gesture of shuffling the cards holds a lot of purpose. It's a deliberate effort to connect to the deck's energies. Therefore, while shuffling the cards, feel them in your hands. Focus on the question you have. If you are seeking answers for another person, use the reflective time of shuffling to ask them questions in such a way that they will understand exactly what they want to know. Ask them to phrase their question correctly and accurately.

Do not rush through the process of shuffling. Take your time to ponder, think, and visualize the question or query. When you shuffle, you are effectively opening the portal that connects our world to the spiritual world. When completely satisfied with the shuffling, place the cards on your favorite cloth and begin the drawing process.

Reading and Interpreting Tarot Cards

Once you have understood the basics of tarot cards and what each of the 78 cards broadly represents, it is time to understand how to read them once you have drawn and laid out the spread—the classic gypsy layout is discussed in the next section. Do not just read out the cards and their meanings. Instead, create a narrative from the interpretations and meanings that each card gives you.

When you first start reading tarot cards, it is often done "by the book" and is a good method for beginners. As you start your journey, you will most likely be using your basic understanding of the meanings of each card to try and read a tarot spread. In fact, keep this book close by to look up the meanings if you are in doubt. You can also write the meanings on the cards themselves for ease of reading. Of course, if you don't want to sully your cards with any kind of writing or markings, keep this book handy.

However, as you read repeatedly and learn the meanings so well that they become part of your heart and soul, you must also harness the power of your instincts. Share your thoughts with the seeker as you pick up and read each card from the spread. Just remember to be kind and compassionate and not use words that suggest doom and gloom. The cards may give us bad news but also give us a way out of difficult paths. So, use that to convey messages wisely and maturely. And most importantly, everyone has it in them to change the path through the choices they make.

The Classic Gypsy Layout

Many kinds of tarot card layouts can be used for readings. We will be discussing the classic gypsy layout, which is a simple one but reveals a lot about the seeker's questions or queries. You can do this for yourself or someone else. It is a free-form spread, leaving plenty of room for flexible interpretations depending on the questions and your instincts.

After shuffling as described above, draw out twenty-one cards and place them in three rows of seven cards each, placing the first one to seven cards in the first row going from left to right, then using cards eight to fourteen to make the second row and again from left to right, and finally, cards fifteen to twenty-one in the third row from left to right. The first row is on top, the second row in the middle, and the final row at the bottom.

Reading the classic gypsy spread is quite easy and is done by looking at the past, present, and future. The top row represents the past, the middle represents the present, and the bottom represents the future. In the top row, cards one, two, and three represent the distant past, and cards five, six, and seven signify the recent past.

Look at the various cards in each of the rows, including the illustrations, derive the meanings of each card from the meanings given in the previous and this chapter—including reversed cards—dig deep into your instincts, compare notes with your questions, and lo and behold, answers will emerge very soon.

Also, you can read more deeply into this spread by reading the seven columns from left (starting from column one) to right (ending with column seven). Let us look at the columns in more detail.

Column one contains cards numbers one, eight, and fifteen and represents the self. These three cards indicate the most critical elements of the current question. Sometimes, the cards could mean the question that is being asked upfront. However, sometimes, these cards could indicate those hidden or obscure but highly relevant questions and related elements that need to be focused on for the current situation to be seen or experienced better.

Column two manifests the personal environment of the seeker, which could be you or someone else seeking answers from your tarot reading. This column consists of card numbers two, nine, and sixteen. The personal environment includes close relationships with family members, friends, partners, lovers, spouses, colleagues, and bosses. These cards show the seeker's relationships with these people in their life, or yours—if you are reading for yourself.

Column three, which consists of card numbers three, ten, and seventeen, represents the seeker's hopes and dreams. It is also the column that might reveal the fears and anxieties of the seeker.

Column four, made up of card numbers four, eleven, and eighteen, stands for the known factors and determinants in the seeker's current state of affairs. These elements could include the plans already in action, experiences that have already happened, or failures and successes that they are already aware of. It also points to what the seeker is currently worried or concerned about.

Column five, with card numbers five, twelve, and nineteen, indicates hidden destiny, especially surprises lying around the corner. When you read the cards in this column deeply, you will likely find impending unforeseen circumstances and hints regarding karmic justice.

Column six has card numbers six, thirteen, and twenty. It represents the short-term future and includes events and experiences likely to happen in the coming few months.

Column seven contains card numbers seven, fourteen, and twenty-one and represents long-term outcomes and resolutions. Sometimes, the ideas and meanings that have emerged from columns six and seven may converge and/or overlap. If there is a complete lack of overlap, it could indicate that an unexpected twist of fate is impending.

Ending the Tarot Reading Session

After the reading session, ask the seeker if their questions have been answered. If you are doing it for yourself, spend a few moments on whether you have got your answers.

If not, gently prod the seeker to ask questions they were previously uncomfortable asking now that you would have built a reasonably good rapport with them. If it is for yourself and you are dissatisfied with the reading, dig deeper into your mind and ask yourself if you are holding back something unpleasant or uncomfortable.

If the answer is still a no, do a reshuffle, and do not hesitate to repeat the reading. Take a short break if needed, and then do a second reading. You might wish to recharge your deck before doing the second reading. It's also good to wait a few weeks to do a second reading. Gypsies often wait for the current lunar cycle to complete before doing another reading for the same person with the same questions.

Whether the reading is done satisfactorily or unsatisfactorily, remember to give thanks to the universe for being with you during the reading.

Chapter 9: Other Types of Gypsy Divination

Tarot is not the only divination practice used by the Romani people. They use many other divination practices, including tea leaf readings, scrying— especially using a crystal ball— palmistry, and others. Let us see how some of these divination methods work.

Tarot is not the only divination practice used by the Romani people.
https://www.pexels.com/photo/gold-kettle-pouring-hot-water-on-cup-of-tea-230477/

Tea Leaf Readings

The practice of reading tea leaves left over in a cup of tea after the seeker has drunk the brew is called tasseography or tasseomancy. The tea leaf reader identifies symbols formed by the leftover tea leaves and interprets their messages. This is a simple but profound method of divination used by the Romany people.

The reason for it not being as popular as tarot card reading is perhaps because it is not very well understood—at least not yet. Let us rectify that mistake and learn some basics about tasseomancy. An 1881 text on tea leaf reading titled *Reading Tea Leaves* by an unknown author, who goes by the name "A Highland Seer," is the seminal document for most tea leaf readers.

Tea leaf reading is all about directing your inner energy to read and interpret patterns formed by the tea leaves left in your cup. Redirecting your intuitive energy is the foundation of all divination methods. When we focus on the leftover tea leaves, they become energy conduits and mirror our experiences, feelings, and thoughts, including the future. When we drink the brew with our mind focused on any question to which we seek answers, the leaves reveal relevant information. These leaves as energy conduits can also offer advice and foretell the future.

So, how does one go about reading tea leaves? The first thing to do is brew a good cup of tea—

although the process differs from brewing tea for usual drinking. You will need: A white teacup, hot water, and tea leaves.

You can use any tea of your choice and liking. Just remember to refrain from using tea from tea bags as their form does not allow for an easy read. Put some tea leaves into the cup. Next, pour hot water over the leaves. You do not have to wait for it to seep because the leaves will remain in the cup.

While you wait for the water to cool down, focus on your intention—if you are doing it for yourself—or talk to the seeker or querent about their requirement concerning the reading. This part of focusing on the intent is intended to transfer your energy into the highly absorbent tea leaves. Your question or intent must be specific because general queries will get you general answers that are often unsatisfactory.

When the water is sufficiently cooled, the querent—whether you or someone else—should start drinking the tea while continuing to focus on the intent. When about a tablespoon of the tea is left in the cup, the querent must swirl and twirl the cup. This is an essential ritual that has to be done with dedication and diligence. Ask the querent to hold the cup in their left hand and swirl it in a clockwise motion.

Next, slowly and carefully turn over the cup with the remaining tea onto a saucer and let it sit in this position for about a minute. Then, rotate the cup thrice and turn it upright, ensuring the handle faces south. If you look inside, you will notice that the tea leaves are arranged all around the cup in various clusters, shapes, and sizes, each of which holds insights into the intention/question.

There are more than 150 symbols that have been recorded in the book *Reading Tea Leaves*. You can use a resource that is freely available in the public domain. Let's look briefly at some symbols that the leftover tea leaves can form and what they mean.

The patterns formed in the teacup are generally categorized into five types: Objects, animals, numbers, creatures from myths, and letters with general interpretations.

Objects — A cross represents blockages. A heart could mean newfound love or improved harmony and love in an existing relationship. A candle or light bulb means new insights and ideas will come to the querent—or you, if you are seeking answers for yourself. Triangles are signs of good fortune. If you see a bed, the querent should take a break and get some rest. Apples are for knowledge.

The sun, as always, stands for happiness and success. If you see a horseshoe, you must make a wish. A sword, knife, or dagger could mean impending danger. If you see tea leaves forming lines, you are chained, or there is an upcoming journey for you. If you see plenty of dots formed by the tea leaves, increased activity is expected in the near future.

Animals — Fish are signs of good luck. Elephants stand for longevity and good health. Birds normally mean freedom, travel, news, or a message coming for you. A bee could indicate that the querent is going to be very busy. If you see a cat, it could be interpreted as some secrets coming to light. Butterflies represent fate. Dogs, as expected, stand for loyal friends. A lion means someone in a position of authority.

Numbers — Numbers usually refer to time. You must read numbers along with the patterns around them because the numbers could mean when something will come to fruition. It could be days, weeks, or months depending on what part of the cup the numbers are formed.

Mythical beings — A monster could mean a deviation from the normal. Seeing an angel could mean that someone is watching over the querent or they are protected.

Letters — Usually, letters represent the initials of people's names. These people are those connected with the query or querent in some way. You should look for forms around the letters that will indicate what role that person will have in the query.

Sometimes, you can easily discern the forms or patterns formed and what they mean. For example, you could clearly see the wings of a bird that could be interpreted as an upcoming successful journey or some kind of freedom. If you see a cross, it could mean blockages or obstacles in the path of the querent's intent.

Further, each part of the cup signifies a different aspect. The cup is divided into three sections for tea leaf reading purposes: The rim, sides, and bottom. The rim talks about the present, the bottom represents the far future, and the sides talk about the near future.

The cup's handle represents the querent's current situation and, therefore, should be placed facing south. The handle is the energy conduit connecting the physical and spiritual realms. Tea leaves near the handle represent events and people in the querent's immediate vicinity. The leaves on the opposite side of the handle stand for the querent's external influences.

Depending on the question, the sides on which the pattern of tea leaves are found can be used to determine the following:
- The timing — how sooner or later the expected event will happen.
- The connection — the distance between the querent and the person(s) involved in the event.
- Intensity — for example, leaves on the rim could mean a life-changing event is about to occur.

Scrying

Scrying is known by other names, including hydromancy, oculomancy, and crystal gazing. Scrying comes from an archaic English word, "descry," which translates to "reveal" or "show dimly." To the uninitiated, scrying is often connected with the image of a witch or gypsy, seeing the images of the future as she gazes into her crystal ball. We need to set this "popular but misleading" image right. Scrying is not about seeing the future because no one can really "see" the future. However, it is possible to speculate and predict what the future holds for querents using current information.

Scrying is an ancient art that allows you to see the future using the current data coupled with your inherent instincts and intuitive power, also called "second sight." Second sight, called variously intuition, instinct, etc., is an inherent human capacity to sense things beyond what our five physical senses show us.

The oldest available text that mentions scrying is a tenth-century Persian text called *Shahnameh*. However, every culture is known to use scrying in some form. A reflective surface such as a mirror, the surface of water, or a crystal ball is used for scrying. For example, the ancient Egyptians used oil for scrying. The Native Americans observe smoke to make predictions.

Here are a few common types of scrying surfaces:

- **Cloud** — Gypsies watch the clouds and the shapes they form to see and interpret the messages they are trying to send you.
- **Wax** — Wax is dripped onto a flat surface, and the shapes formed are observed and interpreted as cosmic messages.
- **Mirror** — Called catoptromancy, the mirror is the most common element used for scrying by modern-day gypsies. It involves gazing into a mirror until the scenes and images merge into one, and some pattern evolves.
- **Fire** — This involves gazing into the fiery flames. Even a flame from a candle or oil lamp will work (although observing the fiery flames from a campfire works best).
- **Eye** — In this rare but effective form of scrying, the gypsy practitioner gazes into the eyes of the seeker to observe the reflections in their eyes and discover and interpret meaningful patterns.

Here is a small write-up about how to practice water scrying.

Considering that water represents consciousness, it makes a lot of sense to use it for learning about and revealing to yourself the power, ability, and hidden aspects of your consciousness.

Materials Needed:

- A bowl made of natural elements such as wood, marble, etc. (brown or black is good).

- Water (preferably from a spring or river, or rainwater).
- Candles (two) with lighter or matches.
- Any small object (a quartz crystal will do fine).
- Energy cleansing materials such as incense.

Use a dark area to perform the scrying. If you are scrying outdoors, nighttime would be perfect. Make sure that you have sufficient space to place your bowl and candles.

Fill your bowl with water. You can collect rainwater if you do not have access to natural flowing water. Tap water or mineral water should be fine if this is also unavailable. Dark-colored bowls help you to focus better than light-colored ones.

Put the quartz crystal inside the water at the center of the bowl. You can use any object for this purpose. However, a quartz crystal is ideal because it has balancing, focusing, and amplifying properties that will help your scrying process. The crystal—or the object of your choice—will be your central point of focus. Use the incense to cleanse the aura of the place and the items of scrying.

When you are ready, light the two candles and place them on either side of your bowl in such a way that the reflection of the flame is visible in the water. Seat yourself comfortably in front of the bowl.

Enter a trance state using any method with which you are comfortable. For a beginner, chanting a mantra or playing a recorded tape of drumbeats should work fine. Close your eyes and focus on getting away from the physical world and entering your mind space.

When you feel relaxed, focused, and alert, you are in an altered state of mind. Now, open your eyes and stare into the water. Be patient because scrying can take time. More often than not, it takes multiple attempts at scrying to see what you want to see.

Now, focus on your intention and let your eyes dwell on the object. Gaze into it and allow the images that form to come and go. Don't try to hold onto any of the traveling shapes or figures. Just stay focused on the bowl and the object in it. Eventually, some clear pattern of words or forms will appear to give you the answer you seek.

Remember, the more you gaze and allow yourself to relax, the better you will access your unconscious mind, the space that holds many more answers than your conscious mind. Scrying is the art of trying to reach into your deep unconscious mind.

Palmistry

The uninitiated and the skeptics quickly brush off palmistry as mere guesswork, as they do all other forms of divination. However, there is a method to the madness of crisscrossing lines you see in your palms because they hold secrets that, if unveiled, will help you lead a more fulfilling and meaningful life. The art and science of palmistry are believed to have originated in India and involve interpreting the forms and lines on your palms. Here are some easy-to-understand foundational elements of palmistry.

The Shape of the Hand

In palmistry, there are primarily four kinds of hand shapes, each of which is associated with the four elements: Air, earth, fire, and water. While your hand might be the shape primarily aligned with one of the four elements, it is also possible for all elemental influences to be present in your palm. Here are the four types of hand shapes.

Air hands are taller than they are broad with upright fingers. People with air hands tend to be highly analytical and rational and put reason and logic above everything else. Often, they come across as being aloof because their minds continuously observe and analyze information and data from their surroundings. They might be sarcastic, but they respect fairness.

Earth hands are usually square in shape. They have fewer but deeper lines than the other three types. As with the reliable and practical earth element, people with this shape of hand are highly dependable individuals. They happily and efficiently take on the burdens of the world. They are not as bothered about emotions as they are about getting things done. They love to work.

Fire hands are normally found on people who ooze charisma and magnetism. Fire hands are often irregular and usually filled with lines. People with fire hands tend to be skewed toward fun and creativity rather than focusing on micromanagement or details.

Water hands are characterized by bony, long fingers and narrow palms, and the lines of a water hand are very fine. People with water hands are highly emotional, almost to the point of being impractical. Yet, they are very compassionate, highly receptive, and flexible to change.

The Three Primary Lines

When you think of palmistry, the three primary lines that come to mind are the heart, head, and life lines.

The Heart Line — The heart line does not answer questions such as the following:

- When will I find love?
- When will I have good sex?
- Who is my soulmate?
- Is my partner cheating on me?

In palmistry, the heart line represents your relationship or love style. The heart line manifests how you like others to relate to you and how you want to relate to others. The heart line tells you how you accept yourself. The heart line can appear in different ways on your palm, including:

It can start from the edge of your palm under the little finger and curve gently toward the index finger. The person with such a heart line usually tends to be empathetic, caring, and giving in a relationship.

It can start from the little finger as above and then dramatically move upward toward the middle finger. People with such a heart line tend to be highly passionate and deeply focused on their desires. They follow their desires passionately and also expect others to know their desires. They are very self-oriented people.

People with flat heart lines tend to have a romantic yet rational approach to relationships. They are thoughtful, considerate, and think very deeply about feelings and emotions. The minds of such people are on a continuous judging program, relentlessly thinking about feelings. People with flat heart lines also tend to appear aloof.

People with a short heart line—one that stops abruptly somewhere below the middle finger—are normally hermit-like. They love solitude to the point of appearing selfish when their sanctuary time comes. They love to work and are productive people. They just like to work alone and be alone.

The Life Line — Unfortunately, most people are under the misconception that the life line indicates the length of the person's life. However, according to palmistry, this is not true. It is the line that shows how anchored or grounded the person is. It speaks about your stability in life and your connections and relationships with loved ones and friends.

- A short life line indicates a hardworking person who constantly needs boosts of vital energy pumped, especially when the person is feeling depleted.
- A person with a thin, faint line could experience chaotic internal tension and feels scattered and lost.

The Head Line — The head line starts beneath the index finger and ends beyond the middle finger. This line reflects how your brain works and how we deal with data and information. There are different kinds of head lines in palmistry. Let us look at some of them.

- People with a flat, clear, and lengthy line are clear-thinking, love to integrate ideas, and love to calculate.
- People with a very long head line—one that is just a little short of touching the other palm—are those who are always collecting data and information, synthesizing and analyzing them. They have hyperactive minds that need to be engaged all the time.
- Those with a long head line but one that is frayed at the end are those whose thought processes never stop. Their thoughts are relentless and so fatiguing that, more often than not, such people find it difficult to reach any conclusion.
- People with a short head line are generally impulsive in their decision-making. They are more skewed toward their instincts and rarely overthink any matter.
- People whose head line crosses to the other side of the palm are usually those who can connect with people who have moved on to the other world. They usually have great psychic powers that help them communicate with gods and spirits. Such people also have problems dealing with the material world.

Mounts in Palmistry

Fleshy areas on the palm are called mounts and correspond to the seven planets in astrology, namely the Sun, Moon, Mercury, Venus, Mars, Jupiter, and Saturn. Elevated and fleshy mounts reveal the person's balanced personality attributes. Sunken mounts reveal the person's weak or underdeveloped personality traits. Extremely prominent mounts reveal overemphasized and exaggerated personality traits. Let us look at the seven mounts.

Mount of Saturn — The Mount of Saturn is situated at the base of the middle finger and corresponds to fortitude, wisdom, and responsibility. It reveals the individual's integrity.

Mount of Jupiter — The Mount of Jupiter is located at the base of the index finger and stands for leadership, confidence, and ambition. It also reveals spiritual connections and divine attributes of a person.

Mount of Apollo (or Sun) — Situated at the base of the ring finger, this mount represents the person's dynamic essence, vitality, and optimism. This mount shows the person's potential for success, creativity, and happiness.

Mount of Venus — Located at the base of the thumb, this mount deals with sensuality, romance, love, and attraction. It reveals the person's indulgence, passion, and sexuality.

Mount of Luna (or Moon) — This mount is located at the base of the palm and beneath the little finger. It symbolizes intuition, imagination, and psychic powers. It reveals the person's ability for compassion and empathy.

Mars — In palmistry, Mars has a prominent role to play. There are three different sections on the palm representing three facets of Mars: Inner Mars, Outer Mars, and the Plain of Mars. Inner Mars is located above the thumb and represents aggression and physical strength. Outer Mars is located under the little finger between the Mounts of Apollo and Lunar. It represents perseverance and emotional courage. The Plain of Mars is located between the Inner and Outer Mars in the center of the palm and stands for the two Mars balanced.

The elements mentioned above are only the basics of palmistry. Once you have mastered the basics, you need to delve deeper and learn about other elements, including granular details such as finger position and shape, smaller lines branching off the primary lines, etc.

Gypsy divination is all about connecting with your inherent instincts to read and interpret the messages sent by the universe through various means. The more you practice these divination methods, the better you will get at gypsy magic.

Chapter 10: Gypsy Spells and Charms

In this final chapter, we will bring together all of the elements presented in former chapters, including herbs, symbols, omens, etc., and come up with various gypsy spells that you can try out.

The more you keep working with gypsy elements, the more magic you will attract into your life.
https://www.pexels.com/photo/tarot-cards-and-a-crystal-ball-on-the-table-7179792/

Healing Spell

Healing spells can be used for multiple purposes, including healing physical sickness and wounds, broken hearts, and even emotional pain. It is important to reiterate here that all healing spells should not be done in place of modern medicine but to enhance its healing power and give the affected person emotional and mental solace so that drugs prescribed by qualified medical practitioners work efficiently.

The healing spell described below is the simplest and almost free of cost. It's perfect for beginners who do not have the money or are still uncertain of the power of gypsy magic and do not want to spend money on spells. The key element in all spells—more so in this, considering that we are only going to use water for it—is your intention.

Make sure your intention is powerful and specific. Here are some examples:

- My migraine is gone. I am completely healthy.
- I no longer feel despair that my partner has left me. My broken heart is mended. I am ready for new love.
- My broken bone is healed. I can move my limbs freely now.

All you need is a glass of water. Use a clear glass for the energies to flow freely. Sit down in a quiet, undisturbed place and hold the glass of water in your hands. Say your intention out loud. Repeat it a couple of times.

Close your eyes, focus all your healing energies and visualize them being transferred into the glass of water. Once you feel satisfied that the water in the glass is filled with your positive, healing energy, it's ready for use. It has become enchanted with your energy. Drink this water and visualize healing energy entering your body.

Protection Spell

This protection spell keeps you—or someone else—safe from dangers. It is simple yet powerful. All you need is one white candle, a candle holder, and matches—or a lighter.

Place the candle on the holder and light the white candle. Next, close your eyes and say aloud the following incantation:

"May the light of this candle,

Protect me from all dangers,

Seen, unseen, felt, intangible, of this world, of the other worlds.
From all directions, above and below.
So, mote it be."

If you are doing it for someone else, use the name of the person instead of "me" in the second line. Say these lines a couple of times, and as you say them, visualize a white protective light bubble covering you—or the querent. Hold on to the visual for as long as you want. When you feel satisfied, open your eyes, thank the universe, and blow out the candle.

Good Luck Spell

We all love to have good luck on our side, especially during special occasions, such as a job interview, a promotion, getting admission into a good college, etc. Here is a spell that can attract good luck during such times. Again, the depth and power of your intention play a big role in the success of the good luck spell jar.

A good luck spell jar is great because you can carry it around—a perfect thing when you need it during an interview for a new job, promotion, college admission, or anything else.

Materials Needed:
- A small, clean glass jar with a lid or cork stopper
- Cleansing incense, you can use any one of basil, cinnamon, or violet
- 1 Green candle
- Chamomile
- Cinnamon
- Black salt
- Sage
- Cloves
- Rosemary
- 3 crystals: tiger's eye, green aventurine, and clear quartz

Light the incense and use it to cleanse all the items listed. As you cleanse each of the crystals and herbs, seek the plant or gemstone's help in getting you good luck for the specific purpose. Create an intention and repeat it as you cleanse the herbs and crystals.

Next, add each item to the jar while focusing on your desired outcome. You can hold each item in your hand and repeat the intention. As you hold the herb or crystal, visualize its good luck energy spreading its warmth into your system. Then put it inside the jar and close it with the lid.

Hold the jar in your hand and meditate for a while. Visualize your intended outcome. Next, light the green candle and melt a bit of wax. Use the melted wax to seal the good luck spell jar even more. As you do so, repeat the following incantation:

"*I feel the winds turning today,*

The wind of luck comes my way.

The skies are calm; there is no storm.

My dreams are true; they will be mine.

So mote it be."

This spell requires a lot of good luck ingredients. If possible, try and get all of the ones mentioned in the list. However, if you cannot obtain them all, try to get at least five of them to get an efficacious good luck spell jar.

Spell for Banishing Curses

The spell mentioned here is one of the simplest banishing spells available. If you feel that things are not going right in your life and believe that someone has put a curse on you and/or your loved ones, do this spell and let the curses out of your life.

Materials Needed:
- Cayenne pepper (a small amount)
- Sage (a little bit)

Take a very little of the cayenne pepper in your hand and add a bit of sage—the purifier. Mix the two ingredients in the palm of your hand using circular counterclockwise movements. Anticlockwise motion is for banishing, while clockwise is for attracting. While doing so, imagine the curse that you want to be banished being eliminated from your life.

When you are satisfied with the mixing of the two ingredients, go outside and blow the mixture out of your hand. Make sure you blow hard so that the mixture is completely and irretrievably scattered, just as the curses in your life. Brush off the specks from your hand and wash your hands clean.

Spell for Banishing Evil and Negative Energies

The spell detailed below is designed to keep evil and negativity away from your life. It is a bottle spell, so you can carry it with you everywhere you go, giving you an aura of protection. Bottle spells are brilliant for beginners because they are easy to make using simple ingredients.

Materials Needed:
- 1 small bottle with a cork stopper
- Rosemary (a handful)
- 7 needles
- 1 black candle

Cleanse and dry the bottle. Add the rosemary to it. Take one needle at a time and imagine all the negative elements and people in your life going into that needle. Imagine all the hatred and jealousy that you are getting and/or experiencing leaving your system and entering the second needle. Imagine all the evil in your body, mind, and soul leaving you and going into the third needle. Repeat the visualization until you have banished all the evil and negative spirits into the seven needles.

Next, place the needles carefully, one by one, into the bottle. As you add each needle, make a protection wish. For example, you can say, "*I am free of all jealousies and hatred.*" The rosemary—already in the bottle—will slowly and surely neutralize all the negativity transferred into the needles.

When you have added all the needles, close the bottle with the cork stopper and seal it. Here is what you need to do to seal it. Light the black candle and let it burn until you have sufficient wax to seal the bottle. Carry this bottle around and keep yourself protected from all kinds of negativity and evil.

Money Spell

Gypsy magic can positively impact your financial health and attract wealth into your life. The money bowl described below will help to increase abundance in your life. It is important, however, to remember that the money bowl is not overnight magic. Money will find its way into your life and stay with you over a period.

Most prosperity-related magic spells give optimum benefits when you align the magic work with the phases of the moon. Start with the beginning of the waxing phase.

Materials Needed:
- A clear glass bowl
- A few coins
- Cleansing incense
- A piece of paper and a pen
- 1 green candle
- 1 candle holder
- Essential oil connected with prosperity (jasmine oil works well)
- Ground or whole cinnamon, bay leaves, ground ginger
- Citrine crystal

Start by cleansing all the items on the list. Cleansing the items will remove all negative energies from the elements.

Then, write down your finance-related intention on the piece of paper. What is it that you want? A better-paying job? An improved bank balance? Make your financial aspiration as specific as possible. For example, you can write, "I have a job that pays me twice the salary of my previous job." If you notice, the example is written in the present tense. That is how your intention should be written—as if you have already got what you want.

You can write as many intentions as you want. However, if it is your first money bowl, make it simple and have only one intention. You can increase the number of subsequent money bowls you create.

Fold the piece of paper on which you have written your intention and put it in the middle of the bowl.

Enhance the power of your wealth bowl by anointing the candle with the jasmine oil before putting it on the holder and placing it over the piece of paper with your intent. Light the candle.

Next, put all the herbs mentioned above in the list of ingredients into the bowl.

Visualize your intention as you create the money bowl.

Ideally, the money bowl should be placed near your front door. Let the candle burn for about ten minutes. If it is not practical to do this, you can place it anywhere safe. After ten minutes, you can put the money bowl in your workroom.

Once or twice a week, when you feel drawn to it, you can add to your money bowl with any of the materials listed above. You can keep feeding your money bowl as long as you want. Ensure your candle and bowl sizes are large enough to last that long. If not, you can create new money bowls.

The spells, charms, and incantations mentioned in this chapter are only simple pointers to using gypsy magic to bring joy and eliminate sadness from your life. Learn and master these quickly. And then, use your imagination and the large amount of information given in this book and make your own spells and charms according to your needs and requirements. The more you keep working with gypsy elements, the more magic you will attract into your life.

Conclusion

Now that you have read the book, you must go back and read it again to put things in perspective. Read each chapter in detail, try and understand what is being said, and what lessons you can learn from it. For example, the stories of persecution explained in the first chapter teach you lessons of resilience, growth, and development.

The Roma did not take things lying down. They fought back, and even when they lost against cruel unfairness and injustice, they did not lie down for long. Like a phoenix, they rose from the dust and started their lives anew, learning and incorporating the lessons they learned into their new lives, yet not giving up the cultures of their ancestors.

Reread every chapter this way, and make notes about the various magical elements mentioned. The last chapter teaches spells and charms using all the elements learned in the previous chapters. Try all the spells detailed in the last chapter, one at a time, slowly but surely. Master them, and soon, the elements discussed in this book will be deeply ingrained in your psyche.

When you have mastered the beginner's lessons, move on and dig deeper into the world of gypsy magic. The deeper you fall into this world, the more you will discover yourself. Keep an open heart and mind, and find a new purpose in your life. Live life happily and meaningfully.

Here's another book by Mari Silva that you might like

Your Free Gift
(only available for a limited time)

Thanks for getting this book! If you want to learn more about various spirituality topics, then join Mari Silva's community and get a free guided meditation MP3 for awakening your third eye. This guided meditation mp3 is designed to open and strengthen ones third eye so you can experience a higher state of consciousness. Simply visit the link below the image to get started.

https://spiritualityspot.com/meditation

Or, Scan the QR code!

References

Beyer, C. (2012, August 11). Folk Magic. Learn Religions. https://www.learnreligions.com/folk-magic-95826

Claire, H. (2018, July 2). How to use folk magic. Llewellyn Worldwide. https://www.llewellyn.com/journal/article/2701

Coles, D. (2020, October 21). An introduction to hoodoo. Cosmopolitan. https://www.cosmopolitan.com/lifestyle/a34115081/hoodoo-vs-voodoo-facts-history/

Savage, W. (2017, November 29). "Cunning Folk": Witchcraft, healing, and superstition. Pen and Pension. https://penandpension.com/2017/11/29/cunning-folk-witchcraft-healing-and-superstition/

Scott. (2016, May 28). Folk magic, witchcraft, whats the difference? Cailleach's Herbarium. https://cailleachs-herbarium.com/2016/05/folk-magic-witchcraft-whats-the-difference/

Shippey, A. (2018, January 19). Who were the cunning folk? — Lord⚥Matria. Lord⚥Matria. https://austinshippey.com/blog/2018/1/19/who-were-the-cunning-folk

Waldron, D. (2014). Folk Magic. In Encyclopedia of Psychology and Religion (pp. 675–676). Springer US.

Wigington, P. (2019, December 28). Folk magic Powwow: History and practices. Learn Religions. https://www.learnreligions.com/Powwow-folk-magic-4779937

Adebare, O. (2022, April 28). Celebrating Black history & Black culture. I AM History. https://www.iamhistory.co.uk/home/10-african-gods-to-know

After life beliefts in voodoo Religion. (n.d.). Haiti Observer. http://www.haitiobserver.com/blog/after-life-beliefts-in-voodoo-religion.html

Alvarez, L. (1997, January 27). After years of secrecy, Santeria is suddenly much more popular. And public. *The New York Times*. https://www.nytimes.com/1997/01/27/nyregion/after-years-of-secrecy-santeria-is-suddenly-much-more-popular-and-public.html

Beyer, C. (2010, February 1). An introduction to the basic beliefs of the vodou (Voodoo) religion. *Learn Religions*. https://www.learnreligions.com/vodou-an-introduction-for-beginners-95712

Cuthbert, M. (2021, September 23). Kemetism religion. *World Religions*. https://world-religions.info/kemetism-religion/

Gleimius, N. (2022, September 2). African gods: Deities, belief systems, and legends of Africa. *TheCollector*. https://www.thecollector.com/african-gods-legends-of-africa-gods/

Kemetic Society. (n.d.). Educationforlifeacademy.com. https://educationforlifeacademy.com/kemetic-society

Traditional African ways of worshiping god. (n.d.). *ATIKA SCHOOL*. https://www.atikaschool.org/kcsecrenotes/traditional-african-ways-of-worshiping-god

Wigington, P. (2011, November 15). What is the Santeria religion? *Learn Religions*. https://www.learnreligions.com/about-santeria-traditions-2562543

Alcamo, B. (2021, October 20). Brujería: Getting witchy in Latin America. *JP Linguistics - French, Italian, Spanish Classes in NYC*. https://www.jplinguistics.com/spanish-blog/brujera-getting-witchy-in-latin-america

Benner, M. (2018, July 17). Curanderismo, the Traditional Healing of Mexican Culture. *Four Directions Wellness*. https://fourdirectionswellness.com/2018/07/17/curanderismo-the-traditional-healing-of-mexican-culture/

Cultural terms. (n.d.). *Curanderismo*. https://www.curanderismo.org/culturalterms

Gomez, S. (2020, July 31). Santería & brujería: Two religious practices embedded in the Latin American and Afro-Caribbean cultures. *BELatina*.

Martinez, J. (2020, September 25). Why more Afro-Latinas are embracing African spiritual and wellness practices. *Oprah Daily*. https://www.oprahdaily.com/life/a34130848/afro-latina-african-spiritual-wellness-bruja-trend/

Padilla, R., Gomez, V., Biggerstaff, S. L., & Mehler, P. S. (2001). Use of curanderismo in a public health care system. *Archives of Internal Medicine*, 161(10), 1336–1340. https://doi.org/10.1001/archinte.161.10.1336

Ruelas, V. (2020, December 21). How brujería helped me heal. *Cosmopolitan*. https://www.cosmopolitan.com/lifestyle/a34979780/brujeria-explained-by-brujas/

Salazar, C. L., & Levin, J. (2013). Religious features of curanderismo training and practice. Explore (New York, N.Y.), 9(3), 150–158. https://doi.org/10.1016/j.explore.2013.02.003

Snider, A. C. (2019, October 11). Bruja meaning explained. Teen Vogue. https://www.teenvogue.com/story/brujeria-meaning-explained

Torres, N., Froeschle, J., Torres, H., & Hicks, J. (n.d.). Cultural Awareness: Understanding Curanderismo. Counseling.org.

Trotter, R. T., Chavira, J. A., & Robert T. Trotter II (Arizona Regents' Professor, Department of Anthropology, Northern Arizona University, Flagstaff, USA). (1997). Curanderismo: Mexican American folk healing (2nd ed.). University of Georgia Press.

Ulloa, G. (2021, October 11). The ancient practice of curanderismo is getting A modern makeover. The Zoe Report. https://www.thezoereport.com/wellness/curanderismo-healing-practice-ritual

Wigington, P. (2012, March 28). What is a bruja or brujo in witchcraft? Learn Religions. https://www.learnreligions.com/what-is-a-bruja-or-brujo-2561875

Wigington, P. (2015, October 24). Curanderismo: The folk magic of Mexico. Learn Religions. https://www.learnreligions.com/curanderismo-the-folk-magic-of-mexico-2562500

Woodman, S. (2018, March 13). What to know about the origins of Mexican folk healing. Culture Trip; The Culture Trip. https://theculturetrip.com/north-america/mexico/articles/everything-to-know-about-mexican-folk-healing/

Allen Cross, J. (2022, April 19). 3 Limpias to turn your luck around. Spirituality & Health. https://www.spiritualityhealth.com/3-limpias-to-turn-your-luck-around

Swerdloff, A. (2016, October 28). How to do an egg cleanse for your aura. VICE. https://www.vice.com/en/article/wnbxnn/cleanse-your-aura-with-the-power-of-eggs

Athame, & Stang. (2017, December 26). Nicnevin: The Scottish witch mother. By Athame and Stang. https://www.patheos.com/blogs/byathameandstang/2017/12/nicnevin-scottish-witch-mother/

Campsie, A. (2019, October 17). 9 charms, spells and cures used by Highland witches. The Scotsman. https://www.scotsman.com/heritage-and-retro/heritage/9-charms-spells-and-cures-used-highland-witches-1404985

Fee. (2021, January 18). Older than time: The myth of the Cailleach, the great mother. Wee White Hoose; Fee. https://weewhitehoose.co.uk/study/the-cailleach/

hag o the hills. (2015, December 17). Traditional Scottish divination. Hag o' The Hills. https://hagothehills.wordpress.com/2015/12/17/traditional-scottish-divination/

Living Liminally. (n.d.). Blogspot.com.

Lou Chaika, B. (2020, October 16). The Cailleach: A witch for our times. EarthSanctuaries; Betty Lou Chaika. https://earthsanctuaries.net/the-cailleach-a-witch-for-our-times/

Scott. (2015, September 7). What is Scottish Witchcraft (or not)? - the role of the wise women. Cailleach's Herbarium. https://cailleachs-herbarium.com/2015/09/what-is-scottish-witchcraft-or-not-the-role-of-the-wise-women/

Scott. (2017, April 24). Who the hell is Sidhe? – Fairy Faith and Animism in Scotland. A Challenge to Divinity. Cailleach's Herbarium. https://cailleachs-herbarium.com/2017/04/who-the-hell-is-sidhe-fairy-faith-and-animism-in-scotland-a-challenge-to-divinity/

Scott. (2019, February 10). Saining not smudging- purification and lustration in Scottish folk magic practice. Cailleach's Herbarium. https://cailleachs-herbarium.com/2019/02/saining-not-smudging-purification-and-lustration-in-scottish-folk-magic-practice/

Smith, K. (2019, August 16). Which witch is which? A history of Scottish witchcraft. Scottish Field. https://www.scottishfield.co.uk/culture/which-witch-is-which-a-history-of-scottish-witchcraft/

Surhone, L. M., Tennoe, M. T., & Henssonow, S. F. (Eds.). (2010). National library of Scotland. Betascript Publishing.

The origin and lore of Fairies and fairy land. (2015, August 14). Eric Edwards Collected Works. https://ericwedwards.wordpress.com/2015/08/14/the-origin-and-lore-of-fairies-and-fairy-land/

Wright, G. (2020a, August 16). Cailleach. Mythopedia. https://mythopedia.com/topics/cailleach

Wright, G. (2020b, August 16). Lugh. Mythopedia. https://mythopedia.com/topics/lugh

Blakemore, E. (2019, November 15). Druids—facts and information. National Geographic. https://www.nationalgeographic.com/history/article/why-know-little-druids

Info. (2019, April 25). Druid. Order of Bards, Ovates & Druids; OBOD. https://druidry.org/

Meitner, L., & Johnson, J. H. (2016, November 14). Humanist common ground: Paganism. American Humanist Association. https://americanhumanist.org/paths/paganism/

The Religion of the Ancient Celts: Chapter XXI. Magic. (n.d.). Sacred-texts.com. https://www.sacred-texts.com/neu/celt/rac/rac24.htm

Who were the Druids? (2017, March 21). Historic UK. https://www.historic-uk.com/HistoryUK/HistoryofWales/Druids/

BBC News. (2015, February 14). Iceland's Asatru pagans reach new height with first temple. BBC. https://www.bbc.com/news/world-europe-31437973

Cragle, J. M. (2017). Contemporary Germanic/Norse paganism and recent survey data. Pomegranate The International Journal of Pagan Studies, 19(1), 77-116.

Dan. (2012, November 14). Norse mythology for Smart People - the ultimate online guide to Norse mythology and religion. Norse Mythology for Smart People. https://norse-mythology.org/

Norse mythology. (2016, October 27). English History. https://englishhistory.net/vikings/norse-mythology/

Routes North. (2022, June 20). Norse Paganism: what is it, and what do its followers believe? Routes North. https://www.routesnorth.com/language-and-culture/norse-paganism/

Wiles, K. (n.d.). Who are the vikings? Historytoday.com. https://www.historytoday.com/who-are-vikings

אמור, א. (2020, אמור, א. (2020, October 21). The Tree of Life and the 10 Sefirot. Derehateva.Co.Il. https://www.derehateva.co.il/2020/10/21/the-tree-of-life-and-the-10-sefirot/?lang=en

Sefirot - Tree of Life. (n.d.). Geneseo.Edu. https://www.geneseo.edu/yoga/sefirot-tree-life

My Jewish Learning. (2003, February 10). Kabbalah and Mysticism 101. My Jewish Learning. https://www.myjewishlearning.com/article/kabbalah-mysticism-101/

Immanuel Schochet, J. (2003, September 22). Jewish Mysticism: Why Is It Unique? Chabad.Org. https://www.chabad.org/library/article_cdo/aid/380317/jewish/Jewish-Mysticism-Why-Is-It-Unique.htm

Kabbalah and Jewish Mysticism. (n.d.). Jewfaq.Org. https://www.jewfaq.org/kabbalah.htm

My Jewish Learning. (2006, October 29). Do Jews Believe In Angels? My Jewish Learning. https://www.myjewishlearning.com/article/angels/

My Jewish Learning. (2008, October 23). Jewish Magical Practices and Beliefs. My Jewish Learning. https://www.myjewishlearning.com/article/jewish-magical-practices-beliefs/

Angels & Angelology. (n.d.). Jewishvirtuallibrary.Org. https://www.jewishvirtuallibrary.org/angels-and-angelology-2

Hopler, W. (n.d.). Who Are the Angels on the Kabbalah Tree of Life? Learn Religions https://www.learnreligions.com/angels-kabbalah-tree-of-life-124294

11 spiritual meaning of cinnamon: What this spice means for your life. (2022, August 17). Naturalscents.net. https://naturalscents.net/spirituality/spiritual-meaning-of-cinnamon-170

A sage smudging ritual to cleanse your aura & clear your space. (2015, March 13). Mindbodygreen. https://www.mindbodygreen.com/articles/smudging-101-burning-sage

Aboriginal sacred plants: Sage. (2013, March 18). Ictinc.Ca. https://www.ictinc.ca/blog/aboriginal-sacred-plants-sage

About. (n.d.). Doebay.com http://doebay.com/wp-content/pages/spices_and_herbs_that_spell_casters_can_use_on_spells_to_bring_love.html

Ancestral herbalism and Samhain: Working deeply with Rosemary. (2019, October 27). The Druids Garden. https://thedruidsgarden.com/2019/10/27/ancestral-herbalism-and-samhain-working-deeply-with-rosemary/

Avia. (2018, March 30). Symbolic mistletoe meaning: More than just Christmas decorations! Whats-your-sign.com; Whats-Your-Sign. https://www.whats-your-sign.com/symbolic-mistletoe-meaning-more-than-christmas-decorations.html

Cervantes-Curandera, P. (2016, October 27). What is the Day of the Dead. Institute of Shamanism and Curanderismo.

Chamomile magical properties. (n.d.). AromaG's Botanica. https://www.aromagregory.com/product/chamomile/

Cinnamon: Spiritual meaning, uses & benefits. (n.d.). Enter The Stargate

Dictionary.com. (2020, December 23). What is "mistletoe" and why do we kiss under it? Dictionary.com. https://www.dictionary.com/e/mistletoe/

Ellis, E. (2021, October 29). Oak Spring Garden foundation - the world's most magical plants. Oak Spring Garden Foundation. https://www.osgf.org/blog/2021/10/25/the-most-magical-plants

Greenwood, C. (2021, September 15). 10 spiritual benefits of cinnamon (love, manifestation, protection, cleansing and more). Outofstress.com. https://www.outofstress.com/cinnamon-spiritual-benefits/

Greenwood, C. (2022a, February 3). 10 spiritual benefits of chamomile (+ how to use it for protection & prosperity). Outofstress.com. https://www.outofstress.com/chamomile-spiritual-benefits/

Greenwood, C. (2022b, May 18). 9 spiritual benefits of mugwort (feminine energy, sleep magic, cleansing and more). Outofstress.com. https://www.outofstress.com/spiritual-benefits-mugwort/

Herb magic catalogue: Rosemary leaves. (n.d.). Herbmagic.com. https://www.herbmagic.com/rosemary.html

Herbs for visionary work at the winter solstice. (2020, December 20). The Druids Garden. https://thedruidsgarden.com/2020/12/20/herbs-for-visionary-work-at-the-winter-solstice/

Jinn, P. (2022, May 25). Frankincense: 5000 years of scent and spirituality. Pink Jinn.

Lets get ritualistic: Frankincense. (n.d.). In Fiore. https://infiore.net/blogs/journal/ingredient-spotlight-frankincense

Magickal properties of mugwort. (n.d.). Grove and Grotto https://www.groveandgrotto.com/blogs/articles/magickal-properties-of-mugwort

Martinelli, S. (2020, May 23). Botanical magic: Plants in Myth and folklore. Three Leaf Farm.

Merry berry: magical mistletoe. (n.d.). National Trust. https://www.nationaltrust.org.uk/features/merry-berry-magical-mistletoe

Michelle, H. (2018, December 21). Mistletoe magick for healing, fertility and protection. Witch on Fire. https://www.patheos.com/blogs/witchonfire/2018/12/mistletoe-magick-for-love-and-protection/

Moodymoons, P. by. (2015, December 3). 10 magickal uses for cinnamon. Moody Moons. https://www.moodymoons.com/2015/12/03/10-magickal-uses-for-cinnamon/

Moodymoons, P. by. (2016, March 7). 10 magickal uses for sage. Moody Moons. https://www.moodymoons.com/2016/03/07/10-magickal-uses-for-sage/

Moodymoons, P. by. (2022, April 4). Using mugwort in witchcraft & spells. Moody Moons. https://www.moodymoons.com/2022/04/04/using-mugwort-in-witchcraft-spells/

Moone, A. (2019, May 28). Magical properties of cinnamon. Plentiful Earth. https://plentifulearth.com/magical-properties-of-cinnamon-cinnamon-materia-magicka/

Morningbird. (2019a, November 1). Chamomile. The Witchipedia. https://witchipedia.com/book-of-shadows/herblore/chamomile/

Morningbird. (2019b, November 1). Cinnamon. The Witchipedia. https://witchipedia.com/book-of-shadows/herblore/cinnamon/

Northern tradition shamanism: The nine sacred herbs. (n.d.). Northernshamanism.org. http://www.northernshamanism.org/the-nine-sacred-herbs.html

Organic African sage smudge stick - Etsy UK. (n.d.). Etsy.com. https://www.etsy.com/listing/835313545/organic-african-sage-smudge-stick

Plants and herbs used for magic. (n.d.). Bluerelicsflowers.com.

Published by J. (2020, February 19). Chamomile folklore and magical uses. Marble Crow. https://marblecrowblog.com/2020/02/19/chamomile-folklore-and-magical-uses/

Rhys, D. (2020, August 12). What is the symbolism of mistletoe? Symbol Sage. https://symbolsage.com/mistletoe-meaning-and-symbolism/

Rhys, D. (2021, June 21). Sage herb - meaning and symbolism. Symbol Sage. https://symbolsage.com/sage-herb-meaning-symbolism/

Ritual tools: Sacred work with Mugwort. (n.d.). Circle Sanctuary.

Shade, P. (n.d.). The supernatural side of plants - CornellBotanicGardens. Cornellbotanicgardens.org. https://cornellbotanicgardens.org/the-supernatural-side-of-plants/

Silva, J. (2021, October 26). 11 Rosemary magical properties and spiritual uses. Angelical Balance. https://www.angelicalbalance.com/spiritual-protection/rosemary-magical-properties/

Silva, J. (2022, July 22). 9 spiritual meanings and benefits of frankincense. Angelical Balance. https://www.angelicalbalance.com/spirituality/spiritual-meaning-benefits-of-frankincense/

Stuff, C. V. P. (2022, October 5). Rosemary spiritual meaning: How to utilize this powerful herb. Coachella Valley Preserve. https://coachellavalleypreserve.org/rosemary-spiritual-meaning/

The druid next door — the magick of Rosemary. (2019, July 7). Tumblr.com. https://thedruidnextdoor.tumblr.com/post/186116542942/the-magick-of-rosemary/amp

What is Frankincense Oil? The Benefits and Uses of Frankincense Oil. (n.d.-a). Saje US. https://www.saje.com/ingredient-garden-frankincense.html

What is Frankincense Oil? The Benefits and Uses of Frankincense Oil. (n.d.-b). Saje US. https://www.saje.com/ingredient-garden-frankincense.html

What is Smudging and How do I Smudge? (2016, June 7). Sage Goddess. https://www.sagegoddess.com/how-do-i-smudge/

White, A. (2022, August 28). 10 benefits of burning sage, how to get started, and more. Healthline. https://www.healthline.com/health/benefits-of-burning-sage

Wigington, P. (2013, May 13). The magic and myths of mugwort. Learn Religions. https://www.learnreligions.com/using-mugwort-in-magic-2562031

Wigington, P. (2014, April 13). Frankincense. Learn Religions. https://www.learnreligions.com/magic-and-folklore-of-frankincense-2562024

Wigington, P. (2015a, October 31). Chamomile. Learn Religions. https://www.learnreligions.com/chamomile-2562019

Wigington, P. (2015b, November 29). Rosemary. Learn Religions. https://www.learnreligions.com/rosemary-2562035

Ibiene. (2020, March 15). African signs and symbols: come learn what they mean.... Ibiene.Com. https://ibiene.com/africa/african-signs-and-symbols-come-learn-what-they-mean/

tommy. (2019, April 18). 16 Celtic/scottish Symbols and meanings. Harreira | Everything Pirates.

Secrets & Symbols: Kabbalah Jewelry Explained. (2018, April 1). Baltinester Jewelry & Judaica. https://www.baltinesterjewelry.com/kabbalistic-themes/

O'Hara, K. (2022, January 10). 15 Celtic Symbols and Meanings (An Irishman's 2022 Guide). The Irish Road Trip. https://www.theirishroadtrip.com/celtic-symbols-and-meanings/

8 FAMOUS NORSE SYMBOLS AND THEIR MEANINGS. (n.d.). Reykjaviktouristinfo.Is. https://blog.reykjaviktouristinfo.is/2021/12/8-famous-norse-symbols-and-their-meanings/

African Symbols: Adinkra. (n.d.). Uwm.Edu. https://uwm.edu/african-diaspora-studies/wp-content/uploads/sites/203/2015/06/Symbols-Adinkra-and-VeVe.pdf

Wecker, M. (2008, October 28). What Is A Hamsa? My Jewish Learning. https://www.myjewishlearning.com/article/hamsa/

Rhys, D. (2020, September 10). Serpent Symbolism and Meaning. Symbol Sage. https://symbolsage.com/serpents-meaning-and-symbolism/

How To Cleanse & Charge Amulets, Talisman, and Charms. (n.d.). Magicksymbols. https://magicksymbols.com/blogs/news/how-to-cleanse-charge-amulets-talisman-and-charms

Coen, C. D. (2022, July 20). Get your mojo working. Weird, Wacky, & Wild. https://www.weirdsouth.com/post/get-your-mojo-working

Huanaco, F. (2019, December 12). Free book of spells PDF: Printable rituals, potions & spells. Spells8. https://spells8.com/free-book-of-spells-pdf/

Lacy, D. (n.d.). Crafty Thursday: DIY Gris Gris bags. Mysteryplayground.net. http://www.mysteryplayground.net/2016/02/crafty-thursday-diy-gris-gris-bags.html

Pham, O. (2022, September 9). Runes, Norse magic, and magical content. Wondrium Daily.

Hardy, J. (2022, July 2). 12 African gods and goddesses: The Orisha pantheon. History Cooperative; The History Cooperative. https://historycooperative.org/african-gods-and-goddesses/

López, J. S. (2021, October 27). Obatala – supreme Yoruba deity. Symbol Sage. https://symbolsage.com/obatala-yoruba-deity/

Ogun. (n.d.). Mythencyclopedia.com. http://www.mythencyclopedia.com/Ni-Pa/Ogun.html

Tabalia, J. (2021, April 22). 12 famous African goddesses and gods with mind-blowing history. Briefly; Briefly.co.za. https://briefly.co.za/48019-12-famous-african-goddesses-gods-mind-blowing-history.html

AA. "Roma Culture Comes Alive With Celebration of Baba Fingo." Daily Sabah

Alethia. "Scrying: How to Practice the Ancient Art of Second Sight (With Pictures). LonerWolf. Last modified August 19, 2021. https://www.lonerwolf.com/scrying/

A Little Spark of Joy. "The Ultimate White Magic Spells List for Beginners." Last modified January 23, 2023. https://www.alittlesparkofjoy.com/magic-spells-list/

Annie. "Gypsy magic: Romani Spells, Charms, and Folklore." Panda Gossips. Last modified July 24, 2018. https://www.pandagossips.com/posts/2055

BBC News. "On the road: Centuries of Roma history." Last modified July 8, 2009. http://news.bbc.co.uk/2/hi/europe/8136812.stm

Boswell, Lisa. "Real Romany Gypsy Life, Beliefs and Customs." #FolkloreThursday. Last modified July 12, 2018. https://www.folklorethursday.com/folklife/real-gypsy-life-belief-and-customs/

Bradford, Alina. "Roma Culture: Customs, Traditions & Beliefs." Live Science. Last modified November 27, 2018. https://www.livescience.com/64171-roma-culture.html

Chris. "Rain Symbolism (7 Meanings in Literature and Spirituality)." Symbolism & Metaphor. Last modified January 16, 2021. https://www.symbolismandmetaphor.com/rain-symbolism-meaning/

Cirkovic, Svetlana. M. "Bibi and Bibijako Djive in Serbia." Academia. Accessed December 1, 2022. https://www.academia.edu/42176038/Bibi_and_Bibijako_Djive_in_Serbia

Coman, Roxana. "20 Superstitions Only Romanians will Understand." Culture Trip. Last modified December 8, 2017. https://www.theculturetrip.com/europe/romania/articles/20-superstitions-only-romanians-will-understand/

The Cut. "How to Read Palms: A Beginner's Guide." Last modified September 8, 2020. https://www.thecut.com/article/how-to-read-palms.html

Faena. "5 Ancient Methods of Divination." Accessed December 1, 2022. https://www.faena.com/aleph/5-ancient-methods-of-divination

First Steps New Forest. "Superstitions." Accessed December 1, 2022. http://newforestromanygypsytraveller.co.uk/superstitions.php#:~:text=You%20mustn't%20cut%20a,can%20only%20bring%20bad%20luck.

Good Luck Horseshoes. "Romany Gypsies and their Lucky Horseshoes." Last modified June 21, 2022. https://www.goodluckhorseshoes.com/romany-gypsies-and-their-lucky-horseshoes/

Grauschopf, Sandra. "7 Lucky Superstitions (and Their Weird Origins)." LiveAbout. Last modified November 29, 2022. https://www.liveabout.com/lucky-superstitions-origin-895272

The Gypsy Haven Online Store, "Herbal Grimoire." Accessed December 1, 2022. https://www.thegypsyhaven.com/pages/herbal-grimoire

GYPSYWOMBMAN. "Colors & Meanings." Accessed December 1, 2022. https://www.gypsywombman.com/pages/colors-meanings

Howcast. "How to Cast a Banishing Spell | Wicca." YouTube video, 3:56. November 10, 2013. https://www.youtube.com/watch?v=OLkdl1k7dD8

Joshua Project. "Romanichal Romani in South Africa." Accessed December 1, 2022. https://www.joshuaproject.net/people_groups/11141/SF

Kelly, Aliza. "A Beginners Guide to Reading Palms." Allure. Last modified December 2, 2021. https://www.allure.com/story/palm-reading-guide-hand-lines

Kelly, Aliza. "Your Essential Guide to Tasseography, the Practice of Reading Tea Leaves." Allure. Last modified May 7, 2018. https://www.allure.com/story/how-to-read-tea-leaves-tasseography

Labyrinthos "Tarot Card Meanings List." Accessed December 1, 2022. https://www.labyrinthos.co/blogs/tarot-card-meanings-list

Lallanilla, Marc. "5 intriguing facts about the Roma." Live Science. Last modified August 28, 2020. https://www.livescience.com/40652-facts-about-roma-romani-gypsies.html

Lam, Hiuyan. "Hamsa Hand Meaning: Discover How to Wear the Hand of God." ThePeachBox. Last modified December 23, 2022. https://www.thepeachbox.com/blogs/jewelry/hamsa-hand-meaning

Leland, Charles Godfrey. *Gypsy Sorcery and Fortune Telling.* London: T. Fisher Unwin, 1891.

Parrs, Alexandra. "Egypt's Invisible Gypsies." Global Dialogue.

Petulengro, Paul. "Gypsy Traditions Today." Last modified November 19, 2016. https://www.petulengro.com/gypsy-traditions-today/

Romaniherstory. "The Ursitory." Accessed December 1, 2022.

Shirleytwofeathers. "The Evil Eye." Hamsa – Sigils Symbols and Signs. Last modified September 24, 2017. https://www.shirleytwofeathers.com/The_Blog/sigils-symbols-signs/tag/hamsa/

Shirleytwofeathers.com. "Magick and Mystery." Accessed December 1, 2022. https://www.shirleytwofeathers.com/Magick.html

Tarot.com. "Tarot Card Meanings." Accessed December 1, 2022. https://www.tarot.com/tarot/cards/

Two Wander. "Tasseography: Tea Leaf Reading Symbols and Meanings." Accessed December 1, 2022. www.twowander.com/blog/tasseography-tea-leaf-reading-symbols-and-meanings

United States Holocaust Memorial Museum, Washington, DC. "Roma (Gypsies) in Prewar Europe." Holocaust Encyclopedia. Last modified March 19, 2021. https://encyclopedia.ushmm.org/content/en/article/roma-gypsies-in-prewar-europe

Wanderlust. "Determine Your Deck—the Many Types of Tarot." Last modified July 8, 2018. https://www.wanderlust.com/journal/determine-deck-many-types-tarot/

Watkins, James A. "History of the Gypsies." Owlcation. Last modified September 26, 2022. https://owlcation.com/humanities/The-Gypsies

Wigington, P. "The Romany Spread Tarot Card Layout." Learn Religions. Last modified March 11, 2019. https://www.learnreligions.com/romany-spread-tarot-cards-4588969

Wright, Mackenzie. "How to Make a Good Luck Charm Out of Paper." eHow. Last modified April 9, 2009. https://www.ehow.com/how_4897274_make-luck-charm-out-paper.html

www.ingramcontent.com/pod-product-compliance
Lightning Source LLC
LaVergne TN
LVHW051916060526
838200LV00004B/166